Developing Children's Behaviour in the Classroom

For my family
Christopher, Daniel, Cadell,
Jemma, Susan and Rebecca

Developing Children's Behaviour in the Classroom

A Practical Guide for Teachers and Students

Sonia Burnard

 The Falmer Press

(A member of the Taylor & Francis Group)
London • Washington, D.C.

UK Falmer Press, 1 Gunpowder Square, London, EC4A 3DE
USA Falmer Press, Taylor & Francis Inc., 1900 Frost Road, Suite 101, Bristol, PA 19007

First published in 1998

A catalogue record for this book is available from the British Library

ISBN 0 7507 0820 4 cased
ISBN 0 7507 0722 4 paper

Library of Congress Cataloging-in-Publication Data are available on request

Jacket design by Caroline Archer

Typeset in 10/12 pt Garamond by
Graphicraft Typesetters Ltd., Hong Kong.

Printed in Great Britain by Biddles Ltd., Guildford and King's Lynn on paper which has a specified pH value on final paper manufacture of not less than 7.5 and is therefore 'acid free'.

Every effort has been made to contact copyright holders for their permission to reprint material in this book. The publishers would be grateful to hear from any copyright holder who is not here acknowledged and will undertake to rectify any errors or omissions in future editions of this book.

Contents

List of Figures

Acknowledgments

I'd like to thank Dr Christine O'Hanlon for her help and encouragement and Wells Park School staff and children who work positively together.

Introduction

Introduction

Picture this; a dark stormy night and a carriage is making its way toward a walled city. The carriage is drawn by two enormous black cart horses. On the front driving seat is Louise cracking a whip over the horses' heads and intent on manoeuvring the cumbersome horses and vehicle. I am standing on the back foot stall with a clear view of the event. Between Louise and I are large boxes containing highly fragile eggs the size of ostrich eggs. The entrance to the walled city is at the top of large irregular stone steps not unlike the sides of a pyramid. The whip is cracked and the difficult task of transporting the fragile eggs in the carriage, up the steps, begins. I direct from the back of the carriage but it is Louise who controls the action. We get to the top and manage the carriage through small cobbled and irregular back streets. We have to deliver the face-less eggs to the right door although all the doors are unmarked.

The prospect was frightening and I am not sure if the eggs were ever delivered. This was a dream I remember best because the imagery was so vivid. At the time I had embarked on a job of being in charge of the Little School in the middle of cornfields in Canada. There were sixteen children emotionally and behaviourally disturbed all under twelve years of age. They were a mixture of syndromes and mental disturbances many of which I had never come across before with my then teaching of two years in a secondary school. Behaviours unveiled before my eyes as I struggled to form a structure in which we could all have common ground. My one soul mate was an ex-pupil whose competence with the children and ability to learn at speed anything I had on offer, amazed me. I knew what my dream was about. I realized that I had frail children who were dependent on Louise and myself and whose hold on realities was as delicate as the eggshells. I could see that our carriage was our clumsy and careful attempt to guide the children back to worlds which they could neither understand nor fit into. We, also, did not know if we could deliver them back into those worlds with which we had no contact.

Behaviour is a complex and infinitely interminable exploration. The road that is chosen to ensure the development of the eggs must be a subjective decision unless it is punctuated by definite signposts and real, informed action. The leader must know what to do in order to make good decisions for the growing children that can make positive differences to their lives. It was no wonder that I worried in my dream. I knew little and all that I learned that year, I learnt from my charges. Reflecting years later, I can see that I built as

I grew but if I knew then what I know now, that dream might not have been dreamt.

My memories of my training to be a teacher consist of an enjoyable period of reading and writing about the Victorian novel, Shakespearean plays and Chaucer. I also remember heated discussions about whether middle-class teachers could teach lower-class children with understanding. In psychology, students and lecturer played a game called 'who would speak first if there were long silences'. No-one prepared me for the reality of teaching or mentioned ideas about how I might convince children that it was more important to listen to me than to each other. No-one explained that I might find children who sat under the desk rather than at the desk. When I observed classes, I found teachers shouting and angry for the most part, and silent in the staff room afterwards. Sometimes the classes were chaotic. But then I also found many of my initial classes chaotic. Reflecting on those first weeks so long ago, I see forty young teenagers with a multitude of difficulties, most or all of which that young teacher was not even aware of. But most of all, I think about the possibilities of my not having been in the position to give the children the help they needed. In a sense, they were my guinea pigs on whom I experimented my budding teaching techniques.

From my perspective now, I cannot imagine any newly qualified teacher starting without the confidence of knowing about behaviour management, behaviour difficulties, related categories and syndromes and developing informed schemes to improve children's learning behaviour in school. After all, the very basis of understanding what we are teaching is not the actual subjects, which is the easy part, but knowing how we are imparting the knowledge and why. We stress to trainee teachers, and in fact to all teachers, the importance of reflecting on the past and improving practice, but we also need to tell them about looking forward and thinking about what is next for those we are teaching and what they will need to develop in their behaviour that will equip them for more complex educative and social activities.

There is never only one way to approach the needs of the classroom, but the important element is for the teacher to possess a background of information to choose from in order to make long-term programmes for groups or for individuals. A teacher should not have anecdotal training that gives him or her isolated response patterning; he or she needs to know how to approach problems creatively within the classroom in order to establish long-term control.

Trainee Teachers and Behaviour Management

The idea of including a much needed course on behaviour management for all trainee teachers has been ignored. It has been a contentious area and most tutors will admit that they recognize its importance but have few ideas about how to incorporate the subject into the curriculum. When I have raised the topic with educators, their response is often angry, or immediately defensive. People know it's important, but where do you start and who is responsible for this area? Any behaviour is a very personal experience and it is a subject that is very close to each person, his or her understanding, experiences and principles. In a sense, we all own a part of it. This is an emotive area where ideas are shared with difficulty and where it is hard to gain a consensus of opinion. Educators have a fear of being prescriptive and with this fear comes a denial of information that could make our trainee teachers and teachers more qualified educators. In education libraries and in local libraries, books and texts available for the practising teacher exist in abundance. These tend to be specific and fail to present an overall picture. College libraries often fail to provide a comprehensive reference to books on behaviour management.

After subject courses, trainee teachers rate behaviour management (Whedall, 1992) as one of the single most important areas that should be included in the syllabus. On reflection, most teachers I meet confirm that help and information about control and management in the classroom was not offered to them in their training. It is ironic that the ancient art of apprenticeship is still considered by most to offer the student teacher the best model of 'how to', and yet two simple criticisms show this method to be flawed. First, the student observes only the teachers s/he is attached to and depends on those models to demonstrate methods of behaviour management in the classroom. In this way, bad habits as well as good are demonstrated and the student does not have the experience to be critical. Teachers as models are not necessarily teachers with specific training and they may still be showing a trial and error method of dealing with problems. Second, the trainee has not been given a variety of choices of strategies to employ in difficult circumstances and therefore finds her/himself at a loss in early practice to the detriment of the children. This also means that the trainee builds not on confidence and strategy but on failure and survival. One student teacher observing that a teacher seemed to use a low voice for control of the children, copied the approach but it failed to produce the same result in her own teaching practice.

I consider that educators must take responsibility for this area of study for teachers. It cannot be squeezed into a fifteen minute space with a ten minute discussion. Anecdotal stories from tutors are insufficient, therefore, tutors should be encouraged to continue their own classroom practice where possible, so that they remain aware of the responsibilities and problems in managing children's behaviour. This would then assist them in their supervision and tutoring of trainee teachers.

Children in the primary schools today need structure from the adults in charge as many have not had the good fortune to develop the language, listening, self control and independence skills through good parenting. It is crucial that behaviour necessary for learning is developed in the early primary years. And in the same way it is crucial that the newly qualified teacher, or any teacher, is aware of the ways in which appropriate behaviours for learning are developed. Many children will exhibit transient learning difficulties, and others more severe problems, and the diagnosis and remediation should be within the scope and control of the teacher.

We should not need to pull in teams of teachers to help teachers with individual problems within the classroom. What we need to do is to train teachers initially and to give them strategies to approach problems even if it is to recognize what kind of professional help a child may need. In the end are we making our teachers professional enough or are we under-training? If under-training, why? My suspicions are that there is a purpose in under-training in that it helps to create pockets of support agencies, educational psychologists and advisory centres. However, it is my experience that these agencies are often over-stretched and would welcome the more informed teacher.

Developing Behaviour Programmes

This book is developed from a course given to trainee teachers and to practising teachers. It does not pretend to cover all facets of behaviour management necessary in the classroom nor does it examine in depth reasons for people's behaviour, or remediation programmes for every kind of difficulty that may arise in the classroom. What it does do is to accept that teachers will confront problems, that they should understand the variety of creative approaches that they may not have considered, or were not encouraged to consider. What they also need to think about is how to be ahead of the problem, not only trying to change what is there already causing problems, but planning how it should be in the next term, or year and how to achieve it. The one most important aspect that will be stressed throughout these chapters is that just targeting a child to change her/his behaviour and giving him or her smiley faces is *not* a programme. All behaviour programmes are for the adults to develop and record, enabling them to put children into situations in which they can cope and learn. Behaviour programmes start with the adults looking at their own behaviour and how they can control it to help a child develop strong positive responses to social situations. A child will only achieve his or her particular targets with particular adult input. This becomes a challenge for the adult and one that few may feel ready to face. The three important related factors are;

- Behaviour does not appear and disappear by magic,
- Adults must be actively involved in the process of behavioural management, and
- Language is the important tool and resource in all behavioural approaches.

Perhaps this is why there is a reluctance for courses to be produced for students. Undertaking this kind of training can be difficult for tutors. It is an awesome task but one that any trainee teacher might welcome. In the end it will be the choice and perhaps the bias of the presenting body as to the content. Clearly this book will present my concerns in training although I will try not to be prescriptive. This book does not endorse any one method of approach and the definition of behaviour management used and discussed in the first chapter should open up the teacher's mind to developing a personal working environment which can help resolve the everyday problems of the classroom. Learning about behaviour is about solving problems.

The book will never be complete, but the interesting point is that the trainee will finish writing the book in their own way as a more professional and thoughtful teacher emerges. However, what it should do is to raise awareness of how good teaching practice can also include a conscious thinking about how teacher and children are responding to this multifaceted problem of education and how we manage to control the environment that allows it all to happen. I hope that teacher training bodies might be braver about approaching the presenting of such information to students as it is, and has been, the one area in which the students and working teachers have demonstrated that they need most help. They do not need anecdotal tales but a real understanding and confidence in their own abilities to manipulate their environments, their own abilities and insights to effect good teaching management and control. Just as the subjects are differentiated so should the teachers' behavioural approaches be.

The words *behaviour, children* and *teaching* for most educators focuses their thoughts towards some aspect of Special Educational Needs (SEN), possibly children with emotional and behavioural difficulties. This is an obvious response. However, behaviour is about all people, anywhere, any time. Information on behaviour is therefore basic to all teaching and relevant to all teachers. The area of behaviour management is just as much about conforming and appropriate behaviour as it is about difficult and problematic behaviour. Sustaining and rewarding acquired social conforming behaviours is important for managing for the future.

Chapter one defines behaviour management as it will be considered throughout this book. It includes basic information about the history of behaviour management but if a more extensive understanding is necessary then the reader is recommended to explore more detailed literature. All therapies have to do with behaviour but not all can be adapted to the classroom. Chapter two is about the creative and practical elements of behaviour management. Here it shows how a token system links effectively with cognitive approaches. The complete token economy set-up may not be possible in all environments but the principles can be negotiated for other settings. How you adapt the therapies depends on how a programme is managed that includes that particular therapy. It is also important to recognize that you can make mistakes when rewarding children. Being positive works, but only if it plays a part in a whole programme that you have devised either for groups or individual children that will grow and become the ethos in your classroom for all. Managing a positive approach is important, it isn't just a decision to say good things to children, inconsistencies can happen unless you consciously and physically know where and how you are developing your classroom controls. In Chapter three it is shown how the balancing of observation and perception plays a large part in making decisions for good management in the classroom. You start by asking simply, 'What am I looking for?'. Sharing perceptions with other adults is a basis for building.

How do you help children to acquire good learning behaviours? Chapter four is about targeting. Knowing how to choose the right targets is an integral part of long- or short-term developments within your class. The focus of this chapter is on the targets and the methods for achieving them. It is the *how* that is most important. The methods are crucial to organization. The art of task analysis is touched on lightly here as a guide in helping you to recognize where a child is on his/her route to achieving a target behaviour. This chapter mentions the fact that often the adults must change their own behaviour to accommodate plans to help the children to change their behaviour. Chapter five is about diagnosis and remediation and how these two come together. The chapter also looks at syndromes and categories and how an intervention sheet might be produced that is easy and practical to use. Teachers should be able to recognize that often behaviour difficulties may be linked to more than just children being 'naughty'. There are examples of how a similar presenting behaviour in five children needs five different targets to work on. Chapter six is about creatively managing the children and their environment in response to needs. Teachers may use strategies but can they change their own behaviour sufficiently to carry out those strategies? Teachers need to make the best use of their energy and become actively involved in the process. What does actively involved mean? It probably means more than just holding onto a class by using a strict regime. Being assertive often means control, but are children being given enough space to learn how to learn independently? Chapters seven and eight look at the important issue of language and how our mode of living has diminished the use of language especially in the pre-school child. There are opportunities for language to be heard but less opportunity for it to be used and encouraged in the early developing years. The important connection between pre-school language and positive learning behaviour cannot be underestimated. Chapter eight is particularly important for the nursery and the reception class. Can teachers work more consciously on language in the early years to prepare children for the 'next years' in school? Chapter nine focuses on the importance of playtime, how it needs to be viewed and how it can be developed. Many schools are removing playtimes, but is this the answer? Chapter ten reacts positively to the idea of action research in schools. It looks to areas that can focus teachers on their own behavioural management with ideas about gaining the children's attention and developing their own classroom initiatives.

Chapter eleven is on how to develop one's own style within and with the help of school policy. Do practice and policy marry up? What help should you expect from those around you? It also explains about statemented children, and reviews in special schools. They are different from main stream reviews which often regurgitate National Curriculum targets, but maybe teachers should be aware of the difference which may help their ability to diagnose problems in their own classes. OFSTED looks to good practice and if nothing else, it focuses people's attention on (OFSTED) how they are working with the children. Chapter twelve presents an overview of the ideas within the book. It looks at concerns that have been expressed by trainee teachers and practising teachers and how these might be assuaged. It is necessary to know the best way to make teachers aware of the changes in attitude needed to develop appropriate behaviour in the children they teach. Who should undertake this task? Building interest makes a more curious and more responsive teacher.

Conclusion

The Elton report (1989) drew attention to the fact that more stress should be placed on the aspect of behaviour control and management of children. So far, the response has been slight and for most institutions the answer is that lack of time and money have made any extra study for teachers impossible. Our future lies in the classrooms and our teachers are short changed. Those fragile eggs, the beginnings, that arrive into the care of those social preparation training centres we call schools, have many different futures that we cannot predict. They are going places that we don't know about, but all of them need to be guided and to be taught how to survive the rocky ride of life.

1 The Family Tree of Behaviour Management

Introduction

Behaviour management as discussed in this text is described in the following way: quite simply, behaviour management means just that, the management of behaviour. The term itself implies a relationship to behaviourism which, in a sense, is true. However, in practise it means more than a behaviourist style of intervention, it also means that any approach or appropriate therapy can be applied to certain difficulties as long as it is managed so that it is effective to the problem. In education, the management of behaviour is most often seen as a programme of positive intervention. It could just as easily mean the management of art therapy as a way of intervening or adding to a solution to a problem. Including art therapy in an overall programme of intervention might be seen as a possibility. It would then be said to be part of a management programme.

Behaviour Management and Cognitive Psychology

Targets, or behavioural objectives and aims, are part of the associationist-behavioural perspective on learning and are an integral part of intervention. Learning and systems theories use objectives to build on obtained objectives. Clearly, a child must learn one thing before being able to master the next. In the same way children with emotional and behavioural difficulties must be helped to eradicate behavioural blocks to learning in order to train up good learning skills and integrating targets into the educational day is an aspect of management to assist the process. The process is not so much involved in extinction, which has the effect of surrounding the child in a rut of inappropriate behaviours, but looking to training behaviours that can stimulate the learning of the new behaviours. Therefore, the behavioural perspective is important to us. Certain good teaching practices come out of this;

- a sense of direction in teaching,
- clearer communication about what is expected from the child, and
- a way of assessing the progress fairly.

Some objections might be raised, for example, the process does not use the stored information a child possesses, or a student is not always motivated to learn by the structured route and it might appear that sideways stepping or pursuit of an interest would not be 'allowed'. These objections are raised by those who believe that the theories in the behavioural perspective do not allow for flexibility within its definitions. They also do not take into account that the child is always building on what is stored but that it is important to recognize strengths and to use them for the future. Therefore, a behaviourist structure is such that it can allow deviations because it knows where it can re-route. It should also be informed enough to use any past information that could be useful in a developmental plan. Whereas it might be thought that the behaviourist perspective deals awkwardly with the above, even if it is creatively used for detour, the cognitive perspective can be included which adds depth to any programme.

Cognitive psychology explains human activities through memory, thinking, problem solving and decision making. The three important factors of perception, acquisition of new knowledge and memory are important in the learning process and to communication. Part of the theory is to enhance meaningful, not rote, learning. However, a balancing of the two should be considered rather than discarding one or the other. Managing, in effect, is informed choice and practical programming. For example, whilst a school may be run on a token economy as structure, its targeting procedure for each child may be based on an entirely cognitive approach. Rote learning in itself has a negative connotation. For instance, learning the times tables does not mean that the idea of multiplication is understood, but for some children routine and behavioural expectation helps to form a safe platform for learning. Rote learning can be used successfully in the social skills areas, too. Either way, the teaching input must include the 'how' and 'what'. In the end, practically, the way we use information and how we behave is dependent on what we understand, and how we understand what we have been told. The importance of social processes in developing cognitive skills only highlights the importance of marrying behavioural, psychodynamic and ecological theories of any kind and managing them.

Learning Social Skills

It is true that learning is not a passive activity but a constructive one. The acquisition of new skills is about effort after meaning. One can see that meaningful learning, built on past knowledge, is positive learning. What if the knowledge and skills are not appropriate enough to be engaged? If a child has attentional difficulties and a deprived and unstimulating background then s/he may need to be aware and understand her/his targets and the rewards and repetition, because somewhere and somehow those good skills must be taught. There must always be an initial building block to a tower and sometimes, basic management is necessary. The classroom must therefore not only be a forum for the continual input of new material but also the place for teaching children skills to acquire material in the first place. It is also important to understand that children, like adults, like to hear information they recognize. When people are confident about what they know and there is a great deal of consolidation, then a person is receptive to learning new information. A teacher may be required to train up listening skills, the lack of which are contributing to poor behaviour, in order to improve learning and subsequent behaviours. Therefore, the management of a listening programme within a classroom of twenty-five, focusing in on three children may need a great deal of programming and class development planning in order to balance needs. The success of a more cognitive process is dependent on building a past of useful and meaningful experiences.

Helping children to meaningful language, to reasoning and problem solving, and good social habits are all crucial to learning and are all part of behavioural management. Helping children to choose, to share and to co-operate must also be managed. Ways in which to co-ordinate such skills can be taken from a variety of theories and applied within any learning environment. The manipulation of these theories, as mentioned previously, and their adaptation to an environment can all be said to be part of behaviour management. An example might be the meeting on Monday mornings between teacher and children. The teacher may be looking to elicit memories from the week-end, and encouraging communication. S/he might also be teaching listening skills, socialization, inclusion of all children into group work, and focusing children into school or classroom rules and the teacher-child relationship. Managing behaviour is about having a consciousness about what you are doing and planning to achieve.

Children with emotional and behavioural difficulties characteristically have difficulties with reading and spelling. Management is about finding out how to deal with that already loaded description. Choosing the place to start is a management process and has to do with the child's behavioural readiness. The teaching of the reading and spelling is also a behavioural management process in that choice of correct material and how to present and reward are important factors. Where the children sit and how can also be explored as an issue of management based on learning theory that is about directing and focusing attention.

Behaviour management is creative and exciting and these chapters are designed to give working knowledge or information to provoke personal investigation and to raise creative awareness of the conscious use of methods and theories.

Historical Facts

Learning about the management of behaviour holds an obvious position in the training of teachers. Or does it? The debate concerning the professional and academic aspects of teacher training has been extensive over the last one hundred years but it would seem that any focus on management and control in the classroom and the art of developing children's learning behaviour has been given only a cursory glance, although fundamental to teachers in whatever sphere of education. Controversy has always reigned over the number of years training may take and the balance between subject learning and practical application in the school environment. In fact, education is still an area in its infancy. We must remember also that just over a hundred years ago, teachers were sometimes as young as 13 years old.

An explanation of the lack of behaviour of management training may be that the fast growth of the multifarious factions of the behavioural field has complicated the way in which a course might be constructed. Attitudes or the presentation of an approach might be construed as prescriptive or omnipotent and teacher trainers do not want to focus on any methods or strategies that may not work and thus mar their reputations. The possible variations in schools, pupils and policies are also so vast as to make the field more ambiguous, encouraging students to discover the art of managing the classroom and following their own leads. While the aim of tutors is not to be too directive, thus possibly laying themselves open to criticism, the trainee and seasoned teachers are left to search for ideas or models of behaviour management with little informed guidance.

In Lovett's (1973) words,

> The educational system entrusts teachers with the twin responsibilities of evaluating and increasing academic performance and controlling and enhancing pro-social classroom behaviour. The unfortunate result has been that significant portions of teacher time are relegated to the task of behaviour control leaving less time for instruction.

A well-prepared subject and organization of resources are great as long as teacher and children can cope with the experience of learning from each other in harmony. This utopian climate can exist but more often can only be gained after a great deal of experience. It assumes that every child is sitting responsive to the subject matter and, given enough resources, is motivated to learn. Recently, more time has been spent asking teachers to grapple with what they should be teaching in the classroom, but the greater part of all teacher energy is spent in trying to deliver the information in poorly organized classrooms and attempting to apply a confusion of anecdotal suggestions for responding to difficult classroom situations. It is small wonder that the teachers complain that they have to be psychologist, parent, social worker and teacher without sufficient training. However, it is true that a teacher's role has always been a combination job. When you are dealing with growing children they have more on their agendas than school work. Twenty-eight four- to five-year-olds may be at various levels of academic and emotional development. The teacher doesn't test the children formally, feed and clothe them or have the means to sort out their housing. To understand the children the teacher needs information about these perspectives of the children's lives, in order to plan for their behavioural development. It always helps us to understand what we do, if we have a background of information which we can turn to in our thoughts, that helps us give educated responses. Fundamental to teachers must be an understanding of learning behaviour however simple, so that a growing confidence in choice starts somewhere.

Use of Behaviour Therapy in Education

Basic also to teachers, must be an understanding of the historical process of the involvement of therapies in education. The growth of this area recently has become insidious and we accept many aspects of behaviour management now as if they have all been in place for a long time. Indeed, many have. Class points and house points used to be part of every school. Children earned points for good work that also earned points for their house thereby providing motivation in peer and teacher respect. It also helped the children to enhance their social conscience. This type of organization became rare as educators became more interested in individual achievement and the intrinsic motivation to learn. Under new guises however, similar systems are being set up as a more open interest in how to motivate children to comply to teacher instruction, and therefore learning, becomes a pressing topic.

Interventions in the classroom must be made with consideration, as they are about managing and controlling a social organization and have to do with the training of individual and group learning behaviour. Teachers will often blame the child for not achieving good behaviour and will cite incidences, carefully putting the onus on the parent or other factors. This may be correct, and it is not unusual for the teacher to be defensive, thinking that criticism of a child's behaviour will demonstrate poor teaching practice. However, the more informed and involved teacher should have a better approach. Coming out with the targets he or she has set themselves, in order to help the child achieve his targets, would be a far more positive beginning. Being able to explain areas in which both the teacher and child are having difficulties and plans for managing the problem is more constructive. A child's difficulties should never be seen to be the teacher's difficulties unless that teacher is hiding an inability to face the issues. The area of positive targeting will be considered later.

A little understanding is always better than none but the ever-expanding field of behavioural research makes study a daunting prospect. It can be compared, for example, to the full works of Freud that more frequently are potted down to appear more palatable to those who need to acquire the gist of psychoanalysis, perhaps as a signpost toward other studies. In much the same way a 'potted' version of some important milestones in thoughts on behaviour are as follows.

Behavioural Investigation

Behavioural investigation, which was paralleled by the growth of the psychoanalytic disciplines, developed in three decades as follows;

- the first decade was more concerned with ideology and the polemics of behaviour therapy,
- the second decade was a consolidation of the ideas, and
- the third decade was characterized by sophisticated methodology, innovative models and conceptual soul searching and a great quest for new horizons.

The first decade might easily be characterized by the simple manipulation of a variety of attempts to react to all the new verbiage and to understand it in various formats. It was a time in which investigation was very practical and was forging new directions for research.

The second decade saw a consolidation, but also a branching out of ideas in an attempt to understand how the theories related to children's development in practice. Approaches had some things that overlapped and some things of their own to offer. The field of behaviour therapy was becoming vast. Some of the basic definitions of branches of behavioural approaches are as follows. These are by no means inclusive but are given here only as an indication of direction and possible further investigations that you might like to make.

The third decade shows the enormous variety and complexity of the investigations in the area of behavioural development and therapy. The route has not been smooth. Varied and complex debates ensued simultaneously, and will be discussed in more detail later in the chapter.

Behaviourism

There are two kinds of behaviourism; one is *methodological behaviourism* and the other *radical behaviourism*. The first is the one favoured by most behavioural therapists and follows a more mental and inferential approach. It includes cognitive processes which are used in most behavioural therapy procedures whereas the latter tends to dismiss mental states. An important point is that behaviourism of any kind does stress interaction in the teaching-learning process. It is therefore not cold and clinical as is often assumed but sets up a working relationship for those involved.

Behavioural Therapy

Some areas in behavioural therapy have particular relevance in the educational setting. Behavioural therapists rely on empirically derived, observable data as basis for clinical and educational decision making. Three areas are important for consideration: a) the target selection b) the treatment procedures and c) effects of the treatment.

Behavioural therapy has been criticized for its lack of ecological or systems perspective. Use of behavioural systems in schools have also been criticized for not giving consideration to the organizational aspects of school, teachers' attitudes and perceptions related to the interventions and the collateral effects of intervention. More recently there has been a move to dispel this criticism by acknowledging the ecosystem and developing the therapy that will complement the structure and the needs of the child or children.

Operant Conditioning

Operant conditioning is concerned with learning that can be enhanced by manipulating consequences and contingencies of reinforcement. It is important to recognize the reciprocal effect of learner behaviour on subsequent teacher behaviour. Vital to this approach is making sure that teacher response is the effective reinforcement that the teacher recognizes as a controlled consequence, rather than one that is controlled by the learner — a reaction response.

Behavioural Analysis

Behavioural analysis is useful when targeting behaviour and its change that effects the learner, the peer group and the teacher. The results in the early days of behaviour analysis techniques that were successful in increasing academic and pro-social behaviour and decreasing undesirable behaviour led to increased research activity in educational settings.

There was slow acceptance of behavioural analysis in school except in the education of the severely handicapped children after early dramatic successes. However, behavioural therapists present evidence that their methods enhance academic learning and teach pro-social behaviour to children and teach teachers to use their own natural occurring behaviour to enhance learning. As educational settings are social organizations, and are about interactions between people, any introduction of new educational ideas or techniques means a change in these basic relationships. This means that the delivery, receipt and advocacy of the system has to be total, and has to take into consideration parents, governors and the community. When problem behaviour arises in a school the natural reaction is for the staff to respond quickly to quell any disturbance and regain the equilibrium. Adopting a more open and flexible approach may appear hazardous and there may be a lack of whole school support for the introduction of a new, untested system which would take a long-term view of behaviour management.

Cognitive Therapy

This approach aims to place behaviour under the child's internal control. Procedures include self instruction training, self recording, cognitive restructuring, modelling and self reinforcement. From Thorndike and Watson, psychology was almost exclusively behavioural until 1960. Cognitive perspectives however were being expressed by Jean Piaget (1955) and Jerome Bruner et al. (1966) who promoted views of active learners motivated by curiosity and learning.

Box 1: A child's view

My father worked with Jean Piaget in the early 1950s. As young as I was, I still remember being overcome by the attention given to me as I pored over cards with various pictures of flowers on them and trying to work out maximum attention procedures. Whilst I remember my agenda, I read Piaget and realise that his agenda was totally different from mine, in a sense I played right into the assessor's hands. When we are children, our perceptions about how and why we do things are not those of the adults. As teachers we sometimes lose sight of the sensibilities of child-hood and knowing this may make us think about how we can enter or become part of the child's agenda in order to make what we feel is important, important enough for the child to learn.

Recently, my father and I were talking at the same conference. I listened as he described his feelings about moving his family to mid-West America. I heard him explain that he felt worried that the political tension at the time and the violence would upset our, so far, tranquil childhood. From my point of view I had a great many other difficulties that had little to do with political unrest. I wore white socks and red sandals and a school dress. Others my age had tights, black pumps, layers of petticoats or pencil slim skirts and I was mortified by my vest at gym time. The children passed me in the halls saying 'pip pip' which at that time I didn't understand at all. They thought my accent was cute and the hardest thing was to be considered different for so long and not quite acceptable for social situations. Children struggle with their own contexts and have a vision from where they stand, not from the height of the adult.

In education, ideas such as providing learners with 'advance organizers' hypo-thesized to activate learners' knowledge frameworks and aid comprehension were postulated. Today cognitive therapy is no longer revolutionary. Its perspectives on human functioning and its concepts are seen as productive. In education however, the cognitive revolution is still in its infancy. It may be that educationalists may see this area as the hidden element of learning and unveiling this element as unnecessary. Within the more specialized areas of education, training up children's cognitive skills is stressed.

Ways in which you put to use theories of behaviour management more practically are discussed later although there is a good chance that you use many daily without cognisance of the facts.

Current Investigations in the Area of Behavioural Development and Theory

Returning to the more recent research in the area of behavioural development theory, two major debates have emerged:

- the possibility of the friendly alliance between psychoanalysis and behaviour therapy.
  This particular debate continues, although a friendly amalgamation of these two disciplines has been reported from many settings. Use of simultaneous psychotherapeutic and behavioural management training for parents was reported by Burnard (1986) as a successful approach for developing a working relationship between the parents and their children who had severe mental handicaps.
- the second debate was concerned with the validity of clinicians' reportage that they claimed they were getting from their data.

This may have been due to the variable and subjective views that may have entered into the process and perhaps an over-enthusiastic reporting to promote ideas before 'real' data was available.

Box 2: Studying human behaviour

In 1958, my family emigrated to the United States where my father was taking up post as first professor in child psychiatry. It is only on much reflection and on joining up early memories with historical facts that the situation that I had been part of became clearer to me. The musical that I associate with these memories is 'Oklahoma'. In particular, I recall the song, 'Oh the farmer and the cowboy must be friends' about the conflict between people involved in cattle. The cowboy had an interest in driving the cattle and the farmers in putting up fences to keep the cattle from wandering and both were unable to see that they needed to help each other in the same game. (Although according to Bill Bryson [1995] these facts of history were all questionable, as a child I believed them.) In the same way, in the late 50s and early 60s the psychoanalysts, the behaviourists and the pharmacological departments were a long way from being friends. The camps in mid-West America were clearly delineated. It is ironic that they were all involved in aspects of the study of human behaviour but at that time, people in these fields were separatists. No members of family could be allowed to permeate another camp. In our family, friendship with children in the behaviourist camp was frowned upon. Friendship with children receiving therapy was frowned upon. Books and literature in the home were naturally mainly in the field of psychotherapies. But as always education steps in. And with the American ideal of freedom of speech and choices, it is school that opened up the other sides of the stories. Most children of all these camps, and my family were

---

no exception, were very much involved in Science Fairs that were open to all experiments and actively promoted behaviourist research. These huge exhibitions from junior and senior high schools seemed to me to be full of pecking pigeons, rat mazes and flashing lights. Being a family in which science played a large part, we children also became involved in the biochemistry departments in one way or another. We all had summer jobs in biochemistry and experimental psychology labs. Psychology courses presented us with options that we had not considered previously. We would not, however, reject the basis to our information. Having had access to those who changed thought in body and mind, Anna Freud, Piaget and others will always be seen as an enriching experience, sometimes rejected as we grew but laying a basis to the discovery of all those other exciting developments in the 60s.

Of course, time changes all, and the recent climate is for co-operation. Cross subject digs are still rampant, denying Freud's influence on the study of human behaviour as an example. But the important factor is the growth of reflection on human behaviour between Pavlov's dog to the genius of Freud's analytic approach, forming a rich carpet of investigation and cross weaving. The exploration has enhanced all other areas of life from literature, the arts, to advertising and business. It leaves education with many choices and the profession should be richer from the experiences. We have all been influenced by the experience. Certainly our family has been. All the children and grandchildren so far are involved in medicine or education and their practices are affected by various branches of the study of human behaviour. However interchange is in comparison, adaptation and sharing of information. Cross weaving leads to further exciting development.

Behaviour Management and Schools

Although behavioural management was initially used to a greater extent within the special sector, particularly with patients with mental disabilities or severe learning difficulties, its popularity moved into all facets of education in one form or another. For instance it was found that rewarding some severely handicapped children with glittering lights helped them to concentrate on feeding themselves continually, or flooding obsessions helped to normalize some behaviours. In some ways, behaviour management was already in education but not verbalized as such. Children were given class marks or jobs as monitors. Once the principles were in place, education quickly saw the possibilities.

My first introduction to a consistent approach to managing behaviour was at a Centre in St. Louis. It was started by a woman who had been a secretary in a psychiatric clinic. She had spent a great deal of time with parents as their children entered the rooms for treatment. However, parents rarely took part in the exercise and would complain that the sessions did not help them to help the child or to improve the family circumstances. The Centre was about combining parents and children working to a twenty-four hour approach. The children had various degrees of autism, some children integrating into main stream schools and some at the beginning of a consistent and positively rewarded programme, and the use of purpose built time-out rooms. It wasn't so much the kind of child nor the patience of the teachers that interested me at that time. The three factors that influenced me were the involvement of parents in reinforcing programmes from school at home and their support of the school. Second, was the kindness that characterized the staff during repetitive and determined training exercises and third, the way in which the programmes aimed at the next stage of a larger structure. Translated in my terms for any behavioural management is the need for the involvement and support of all adults, an understanding of why and how programmes are developed and where they are going in the best interests of the needs of the child.

Cultural Attitudes to Psychoanalytical Approaches to Behaviour

In the United States progress continued within all kinds of educational environments with a blossoming of creative branches of therapeutic approaches.

In England, the influence of the psychoanalytic approaches although not immediately accepted, became what seemed a more understandable approach for many. Psychotherapeutic approaches to children with emotional and behavioural difficulties were at first questioned and as there were no other approaches on offer, it became a norm. Perhaps the ideas seemed to have, in post-war years, a 'human' feel to them. People in England were anxious about behavioural methods and still are for the most part. They feel that behaviour management is cold and clinical and that it 'bribes' children. The idea that it can provide an arena for caring relationships is still not entirely understood. In education, using behavioural management ideas was all right as long as they were not named as such. To some extent this idea remains true in both the training of teachers and within some schools. The term that seems to be preferred is discipline which implies a hard-line control, defined in the dictionary as punishment intended to correct crimes or errors, the enforcement of rules, to teach obedience.

The growth of a creative use of management, openly discussed within education has been stunted until more recently perhaps by the confusion in people's minds between managing behaviour and discipline that as an enforcing word seems to suggest more immediate results. With the rise of difficult behaviours in the classrooms, the idea of the tightening of discipline seems to assuage people's unease because they understand what it means. How effective the training of obedience is and whatever connotations it carries over the long term for children and school policy is not considered.

Criticism of behavioural approaches are invalidated by the following:

- behaviour therapy is neither a superficial nor a symptomatic form of treatment,
- behaviour therapy as currently practised is not an approach that rejects or even de-emphasises the importance of cognitive processes and other covert processes, and
- behaviour therapy is neither mechanistic nor impersonal.

Creative and Scientific Aspects of Behaviour Management

Della Fish (1988) presents a list of the differences between the scientific and the artistic approach. We can use it to help us to understand why people think behaviour management is a science and how it is also an art form, a creative process. The area is as artistic as it is scientific and therefore blends well into the classroom. Perhaps its strength is in its ability to be amoebic in form in that educative situations can be *managed* and *analysed* whether they are with or without rules, about exploration, about the patterns of human behaviour, or about trying out new meanings or understandings. It is knowing of the artistic and scientific aspects that makes a good behaviour manager.

Science versus Art

- Science seeks rules, principles, laws: Art starts where rules fade and prefers guides,
- Science uses diagnosis, analysis, prescription: Art offers interpretation, exploration,
- Science uses schedules, follows detailed pre-planning: Art prefers rules of thumb, spontaneity,
- Science offers the learner mainly skills and information: Art sees learning as better facilitated by means of structure and patterns,
- Science rests on routines: Art moves quickly to improvisation,
- Science demands closed, efficient systems: Art provides room for imagination. (N.B. This is not to say that creativity and imagination are absent from science),
- Science can reduce all learners to the same by stressing the similar aspects of routines: Art will increase the differences by stressing individual interpretation and creativity,
- Science uses task analysis to help determine what the learner will need: Art suggests imagining yourself as the learner,
- Science sees people as puppets and receivers: Art sees people as negotiators of new meanings and understandings,
- Science talks about motivation, feedback, 'failed input': Art talks about how humans react and respond,
- Science sees learning as stemming from efficient teaching: the Arts see learning as not actually logically related to teaching at all,

- Science sees knowledge as static, attainable absolute: Art sees knowledge as temporary, dynamic, only able to be grasped at,
- Science bases knowledge about teaching and learning on the scientific disciplines of psychology, sociology and linguistics: Art bases such knowledge on understandings gleaned from art, literature, history and philosophy,
- Science assumes (Ed.) theory is scientific theory: the Arts allow such theory to be person-created via a mixture and range of humanities including literature, art, history, autobiography, and certain approaches of sociology,
- Science refers to aims, behavioural objectives: Art prefers intentions and goals,
- Science talks about feedback tools: the Arts prefer the ability to read about other human beings and their actions and to work with rather than on them,
- Science prefers prescriptions: the Arts offer guides,
- Science brings to education thinking as atomising and analytical approach: the Arts function by means of critical appreciation.
  (Fish, 1988, p. 65)

Courses often offer an approach to behaviour that is creative, but on attendance, don't quite fulfil their promise. It is difficult because creativity is often individual, and the ability to find ways to develop programmes is dependent on the way in which any one educator may think. Delineating art and science is questionable but may be useful here. The principle of behaviour management particularly in educational terms is that the manager can create a structure within the environment and develop programmes that will enable both adults and children to work together, to teach and learn to the best of their ability. Rules may be created but they will vary from environment to environment. Variability of needs of the children mean that the adult has a variety of strategies and options but how these are implemented is an educated choice.

The importance of planning   Whilst we shall see that diagnosis of the problems plays a major part in the management of behaviour and the analysis of the whole picture, there is still a great deal of scope for exploring new avenues in managing that behaviour.

Observation of behaviour should be objective in order to create workable and readable programmes but this does not rule out subjective interpretations that may have a great deal of bearing on the way in which a programme is sustained. For example, you may see that a child is being spiteful up to six times a day but you may also feel that the child is frustrated by the need to be a leader but not knowing how to become one more openly. There is no substantial evidence to support your interpretation other than your own experiences. And whilst subjectively excusing the behaviour, you might be able to incorporate your own feelings about the 'why' into a management programme that develops leadership qualities as well as a language for the child to use with her/his peers as an alternative to spiteful behaviours.

It is important for the plans to develop over time. After all, children are forever developing and at a rate that is not noticeable day to day, therefore educators need the insight to work with the individual's development and to recognize that they are working alongside many other concurrent physical, academic and social changes.

Behaviour management works with observable skills and known information but the ability to programme depends heavily on structures and patterns. Without the knowledge of patterns, divergence would not be recognized. However, it may be true to say that improvisation whilst excellent for music lessons, would not rate as highly in the management of behaviour. Reaction on the spur of the moment is not a positive addition to control. By and large it is the immediate reactions to problems that can aggravate and extend the problem. It might be said that the new teacher is prone to improvisation leading to stress and upset as problems worsen.

Imagination Management works best when it is efficient but efficiency should not exclude imagination. In fact, imagination often comes first and it is how the imagination is used in designing workable plans that helps keep up motivation and a consistent approach to the programmes.

When thirty people in a room have to learn a variety of subjects, move about, share resources, listen to each other, look at artefacts at the same time, remain as individuals but follow the same rules in the same ways, then there is a need for routines that are understood and good social skills. All learners must be able to learn together but it does not mean that they will be the same. They will intake information with what tools they each have but management is about creating a milieu that allows them to do so. Behaviour management is about routines but it is also about differentiation. Just as work can be differentiated then so can behaviour. The teacher may have the highest expectations for all children to succeed and be receptive to the best of his or her ability, but for example, attention spans can vary and it is working within the differences and improving on them that makes management of the individual as important as the management of the group. Task analysis is a tool for the teacher. It helps to formulate 'what is next' for each individual child. We are, all of us, continual learners and within art and science, analysis helps us to understand something new.

Talking about behavioural skills in class Where I am working, the children are asked to be able to verbalize their behaviours. They are asked to talk about behaviours that show that they have thought about sharing, co-operating and managing their own responses to situations. They are also asked to understand the tools that are used to help direct their behaviours in social situations and then to understand how to control and take charge of their own behaviours. In this sense they are negotiators of new meanings and understandings.

Behaviour management combines the art and science by talking about motivation, about feedback but also about acquiring a consciousness about how humans react and respond. Behaviour management is about good teaching practice and that includes the most basic element of teaching children the skills used in learning. Behavioural skills are essential to learning and to the enactment of art. These include listening, looking, being motivated, attending to a task, raising interest and awareness, sharing information, sitting with peers, responding to questions and treating resources and people with respect. Most activities in the classroom need the above behaviours in some form or another and most train up those skills. I think it may be true to say that most artists would agree that a great deal of learning is needed to understand an involvement in art.

Behavioural targets   Most behavioural targets for children are placed within their grasp. Children need to be confident about their ability to manage themselves and need to see their own successes, hence the fact that if a child has big problems, small steps are best toward achievement. If a child never follows a group direction, a teacher can start by making sure that a small direction is achieved first. Should this child always drop a pencil on the command of 'Put your pencils down', make sure that s/he has to collect the pencils at the table and give them to you before you give the command for all the children. This way all the children can be praised for doing the right things. The greater aim may be to build up in the child a sensibility about doing the right things and being praised for them. Nothing can be temporary and just grasped at when an individual is growing and learning. Some behaviours are learned, and then change. It is thought that the former behaviours are obsolete, have disappeared, but no, they have all been part of a process and are still ingrained and are part of new behaviour patterns. An example of this is the art of learning to play in nursery. The rules of play are the same as the rules in school and in work and then can be taken back to the family to train up the next generation. The resources change, the environment changes but the lessons learnt are there forever. We need to consider what happens if those early rules are not present, the opportunities not available, or the role models are unsociable.

Learning about behaviour — a continuing process   Learning about behaviour is something we all do all the time. We talk about people — what they do, how they do it, when they do it. We watch behaviours on the television, in theatre, on films. They are described to us on the radio, in books, in magazines and comics. We laugh at some behaviours and commiserate with others. We look at behaviour depicted in pictures, we try to understand the behaviour of our ancestors in history and we try to verbalize and reason out the meanings behind what we do and see. Those who manage behaviour are not just those who have read about psychology, sociology or linguistics. They are people who consciously learn about behaviour from all aspects of life available to them. Making decisions about how to manage behaviour is not one to be taken lightly and narrowly. You might just as easily learn about how people behave from the point of view of Thomas Hardy as from John Updike or Mary Wesley. We all have something to say about behaviour. We need to know, to experience, and to learn about behaviour and balance that with the scientific methods.

Prescriptive Theories

Prescriptive may be scientific but it is also this factor that frightens many educators. In a sense, many behaviourists put forth theories that are prescriptive. *What has worked for me may work for you.* Sometimes those theories can be flexible enough for success in other environments. Knowing what they are, however, is important in that there is an abeyance of information that a trainee teacher may like to call on in the future. For instance, the positive approach is a good strategy. Positive rewards are more likely to be effective than negative attentions. However, a teacher will feel very hard pressed to make this practice continual day in and day out. Like all theories, they need to be placed within a working environment and given a place in a process where they can be most effective. Behaviour management today requires an involvement in teaching that changes the focus of the teacher from an individual who responds to stimuli to managing processes. After all isn't this what growing up is all about?

Contemporary Understandings of Behavioural Management

In returning to the elements of the behavioural approach we must recognize that historically behaviour therapists share the following;

- focus on current rather than historical determinants of behaviour,
- emphasis on overt behaviour change as the main criterion by which treatment is to be evaluated, and
- specified treatments that can be repeated.

But the modern therapist might also:

- look at a total picture of the child which includes historical perspective,
- talk about managing the developmental process rather than changing behaviour, and
- talk about generalizing areas in which treatments can be repeated.

From this understanding, it is easy to fit a behavioural approach into the arena of education for managing in the classroom. Understanding is the operative word. If adults recognize the total picture then various ideas for control can emerge with more confidence. Popular at present is the idea of the classroom as an ecosystem in which every change within a system affects its balance and that balance should be continually redressed.

Current Theories in Behavioural Investigation

Behavioural investigation and its theory broke into factions during the last three decades and has developed even more branches in the last ten years.

In Fig. 1.1 below are some of the basic questions and statements about behavioural management. The interest factor is that most teachers would be able to give examples within their own teaching for most of these statements but perhaps have not equated the practical application to basic theory.

And so what else do we need to know but perhaps do not need to verbalize? What overall behavioural principles should exist that may lead to developing children with positive learning behaviour?

- to be concerned with observable behaviour
- to assume that all behaviour is learned
- to accept that learning involves changes in behaviour
- to know that learning is followed by something good
- to recognize contexts — people behave in different ways in different settings

Reinforcement of Positive and Negative Behaviours

Reinforcement is considered the most important principle of learning. Reinforcement is used to shape and build desired goals. What is a reinforcer? Whatever you can think of basically that gets the right response. These reinforcers can range from spinning a top, a hug, smarties, a smile, watering plants, first in line, taking a message, play with friends, choice of pudding, a new pencil, a token, anything as long as the adult pays attention to the moment and treats the reinforcer with respect. A reinforcer is never the end of the line, the adult must know what comes next and so should the child. When we look at targeting, you will realize that the target is always part of a greater plan. Reinforcers are part of what model?

Operant Conditioner Model

A reinforcer is something that follows a response and increases the likelihood of the occurrence of that response. Doing the right thing gets a positive response. More common for all of us daily would be praise, attention, food, water, sex, pay check — or in school; tokens, good work stickers, toys, tuck, shop, extra privileges, special activities and you can probably think of more. If a child is looking for attention, as all children (and all adults) do, can s/he be trained into a better way of gaining that attention? Give it to him/her! Most people think that they are using systematic rewards more frequently than

Figure 1.1: Questions and answers — chart shows the basis to thought that developed current practice

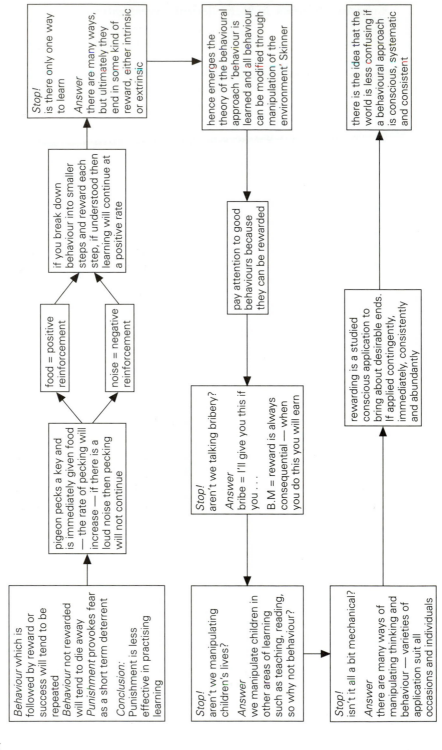

Behaviour which is followed by reward or success will tend to be repeated
Behaviour not rewarded will tend to die away
Punishment provokes fear as a short term deterrent

Conclusion:
Punishment is less effective in practising learning

pigeon pecks a key and is immediately given food — the rate of pecking will increase — if there is a loud noise then pecking will not continue

food = positive reinforcement

noise = negative reinforcement

if you break down behaviour into smaller steps and reward each step, if understood then learning will continue at a positive rate

Stop!
is there only one way to learn

Answer
there are many ways, but ultimately they end in some kind of reward, either intrinsic or extrinsic

hence emerges the theory of the behavioural approach 'behaviour is learned and all behaviour can be modified through manipulation of the environment' Skinner

pay attention to good behaviours because they can be rewarded

Stop!
aren't we talking bribery?

Answer
bribe = I'll give you this if you . . .

B.M = reward is always consequential — when you do this you will earn

Stop!
aren't we manipulating children's lives?

Answer
we manipulate children in other areas of learning such as teaching, reading, so why not behaviour?

Stop!
isn't it all a bit mechanical?

Answer
there are many ways of manipulating thinking and behaviour — varieties of application suit all occasions and individuals

rewarding is a studied conscious application to bring about desirable ends. If applied contingently, immediately, consistently and abundantly

there is the idea that the world is less confusing if a behavioural approach is conscious, systematic and consistent

Figure 1.2: Behavioural approaches for positive teaching

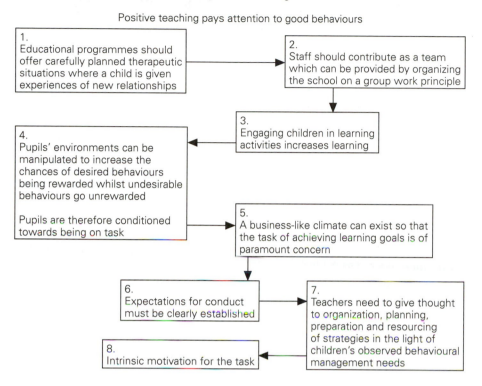

Positive teaching pays attention to good behaviours

1.
Educational programmes should offer carefully planned therapeutic situations where a child is given experiences of new relationships

2.
Staff should contribute as a team which can be provided by organizing the school on a group work principle

3.
Engaging children in learning activities increases learning

4.
Pupils' environments can be manipulated to increase the chances of desired behaviours being rewarded whilst undesirable behaviours go unrewarded

Pupils are therefore conditioned towards being on task

5.
A business-like climate can exist so that the task of achieving learning goals is of paramount concern

6.
Expectations for conduct must be clearly established

7.
Teachers need to give thought to organization, planning, preparation and resourcing of strategies in the light of children's observed behavioural management needs

8.
Intrinsic motivation for the task

punishment. Recent observations in a special school showed that teachers were surprised that when they had thought they were praising and keeping children on-task, their praise had been far less than their reprimands. Strangely, the teacher/adult feels rewarded by the child who is working well, as if this were merely a reflection of good practice and therefore s/he does not remember that it is the child who needs rewarding. For example, the child who is quietly working may be ignored unconsciously by the teacher but if he starts to create a problem, the adult will reprimand. It may be that if the child is quick to respond, the teacher or adult is unlikely to recognize his or her own negative input. However, in the long term, the child's attention to task may deteriorate and the adult would more often look to the child's problematic behaviour but not the adult's behaviour. Although that particular observation noted above showed a 99 per cent attention to task, over the week attention to task was inconsistent. A teacher then concentrating on more consistent praise noted a better attention to task over several weeks. Teachers should be aware that they are training children for the next stage, next class, next teacher, new learning. If they reward children for on-task behaviour, then the children are more likely to sustain their behaviour for the next thing. A teacher should look to training up the sense of intrinsic reward in the child, once s/he is confident that the child feels consistently motivated.

Extinction

Extinction is ignoring positive or negative behaviours. This has the effect of not reinforcing and therefore not sustaining positive behaviours, or more importantly not reinforcing negative behaviours enough to sustain them. Teachers are reluctant to attempt extinction for fear of either a loss of control or being observed not to be dealing with inappropriate classroom behaviours. With large class sizes, they also fear children using peers as models and exacerbating and extending the behaviours. However, it is possible under control situations to manage the idea of extinction within the classroom. Control situations may be when the adult has particularly decided on a time during the week, with a particular attentional exercise, to praise and stimulate good listeners as models for the children who have difficulties when in a group.

Punishment

Punishment is used verbally frequently with threats of contingencies which range from missing the good class times to exclusion, although it has been found that it has very few learning outcomes. Punishment is negative consequences, removal of privileges or desired activities. Fear of the punisher is the only deterrent. The danger is that punishment always gets greater. It has a way of separating children from their peers and away from situations in which they should be learning to cope. It can only be used in a situation if it is part of a programme that allows a child to earn back what he/she has lost.

Modelling

Modelling phenomena is a very strong tool. Watching all behaviour is a learning process for children. It is therefore important in the creating of strong positive group working situations that children joining can quickly recognize as acceptable ways in which the system works. Teachers and other adults are important to children. Children, most often primary and junior children are known to copy teachers' intonations, habits, and styles of social approach.

Box 3: Building a life

When an architect builds, he has to know basic facts about the kinds of soils, about the strengths of materials, about the environment and about what kind of people will be using the buildings. S/he then produces a blue print of the shape of the building and then focuses on specific areas, on finite details. S/he must know what resources are available and in what quantities. S/he needs to look ahead to future use and development of the building. People then come together to work as a team to put the

---

plan into operation. For this, good attendance, support and co-operation are needed. The foundations must be deep enough and strong enough to support growth. Each section has to meet with others to make connections for the next stages. Then the building has to be tried out. The architect moves away from the situation and the meaning of the building is consolidated by its use. There may be some problems to start with and as time goes on, these are ironed out and the building becomes part of lives and the community. The architect then needs to reflect on the process, s/he rationalizes its position, its shape and its use. We usually say that the work of the architect is creative. However, a great deal of the work is the production of the plans which means a lot of measuring and line drawing, these days computer led. Changes in resourcing should not change the quality of construction. S/he must know what kind of people will be in the building, what they will do and how they will do it. Irrespective of the contribution, the architect can see what is produced and the end product can stimulate opinion and discussion.

When a teacher teaches, basic facts, knowledge of resources and planning, use of the environment and knowing the children and their particular needs are all essential to the job. A teacher is not building buildings although may vicariously have a hand in it, but is part of the building of an individual. Whereas many people will use one door and recognize its use, the tools a teacher uses will have various effects on various people. Whereas the plan of the architect is seen in actuality, the programme a teacher might make to develop a child's behaviour will continue to develop as the child develops and the growth of the child will be the sum of many factors, all of which no one person will know. Many bricks make a building but in the end the product will be understood by many and will be describable to most. In teaching the end product will still be a mystery — the parts of a person never totally understood or contributed to by any one person. As teachers we must recognize that we are builders and we have a responsibility to the future of each individual. Our foundations must be deep enough and strong enough to help individuals grow in ways that make social connections with the world they live in. Our ideas and our programmes and our reflections are important to the future of the next child. Also important are basic understandings that we should all have about how people learn, what they need to learn and how you will make those things happen. Unlike the architect, there is no end product and to this extent the field of education is not spoken of as being a creative profession although people may speak of individual teachers as being creative. Education does not have an end product as it starts a development that will go on as a process over a lifetime. Yet education is a creative profession and we need to develop a consciousness in our teachers about the art of teaching without the over-use of the Gradgrind model.

Conclusion

Behaviour management is about co-ordinating what we know about behaviour, the process of development, what will redirect difficult behaviours, about looking ahead and planning creatively for the group and for the individual. Teachers should first of all know what learning behaviours children need to have before they start a task. These entry skills are as important as preparing resources and planning areas of the curriculum. We need to be aware as teachers that being a professional is about knowing about learning behaviour and how to control, manage and create it. This is not extra to a teacher's role, it is essential to it. At present, the consideration of management in training is given lip service. However, it is clear to both practising and trainee teachers that for the former managing behaviour is an area they should have been well trained in and for the latter it is the greatest fear that he or she will not be able to manage the children. The teacher who is informed with historical evidence, strategies, and understanding of how children acquire adequate learning behaviours especially disruptive pupils, will have more confidence and be able to demonstrate good practice.

2   Practical Use of Therapies

Introduction

Many years ago I was teaching in a small school for the maladjusted. Next door to my classroom, was a teacher with six difficult children. So difficult in fact, that they seemed to take apart the classroom and the contents and to leave the room in a state of total chaos and disrepair. Most of the children could not recognize their letters and all of the children were very physical and abusive. The class assistant spent most of the day with one arm across the doorway to stop the children leaving the classroom. No teaching took place — only containment. I had my own worries at the time. I had the youngest very active class and I was involved in getting their reading off the ground and getting to grips with their behaviours. The school had little policy at that time, it was a sink or swim situation and a 'send you to the all forgiving head' if things get too bad. The teacher next door left in the middle of the year and I was asked to take over the class. It was easy to prepare the class, everything went out to the rubbish except just enough tables and chairs. I decided that as soon as the children walked in the new regime would start. The class assistant was relieved of her job as bouncer and given particular jobs to do. What next? How does one start to manage? What decisions do you make about what strategies to use? How do you make children respect a room and environment that has meant very little? Where do you start teaching and what to teach? No-one told me I would be faced with this in teacher training. I am not a bully myself, so threatening adult behaviour is not my style. How I remediated the situation, using some of the strategies and therapies mentioned here, is continued at the end of the chapter.

Managing Behaviour

In an average day, a classroom teacher may use any number of strategies, sometimes consciously, sometimes unconsciously. The following example shows the variety of strategies that could be used in a simple situation:

The teacher lines children up to enter classroom. When not all the children comply, s/he:

- calls on the child who is standing quietly and attentively to be in the front,

- calls the children to attend to those who are making them line up for longer than necessary,
- removes the children not managing from the line and asks the others to file in,
- shouts at the children to be ready,
- talks quietly to the children about what is and will be expected of them in the classroom,
- picks out the children who are looking good and explains that they will have first choice of activity,
- explains that all children will practise lining up during their playtime,
- ignores the children not lining up as asked and takes them all in anyway, and
- has already appointed a leader for the front of the line (incentive).

These are all examples of managing behaviour. Which examples do you think will mean that the children will line up well tomorrow? Can you substantiate your choice?

Practical Behavioural Strategies for the Classroom

Particular syndromes and categories of problematic children will be looked at later, where we will look deeper into factors that may affect learning such as the psychiatric syndrome, the intellectual level and its significance, associated biological factors, psycho-social factors and developmental disorders. Here is a list of behaviours simply as you may see them in the classroom followed *by* the *strategy* you might adopt:

1   not listening to directions
2   talking when asked not to
3   fidgeting
4   calling out
5   not attending to task
6   'tells' on other children
7   bullies other children
8   out of seat
9   annoying other children
10   destroying work and other children's work
11   solitary in class and play
12   poor concentration, short attention span
13   stealing in class
14   refusing to try new tasks

Creating a behaviour management programme that is both personal to you and your abilities is about having options to consider. These options, without knowledge of children or environment, might be any one of the following responses. At this moment you will only be able to consider a consistent response to the actual problem that you might be happy with. Later on you may think of other strategies that might help the child over a much longer period of time which will mean that these examples will form part of a programme. The following demonstrate strategies which concern both teacher and pupil behaviour to use with behaviours as in the above list:

1. *Children do not always listen well to adults.* Give the directions orally to all children. Break down the directions and make sure that each section of the directions is completed by each child. Use a resource for the children to look at and make sure that all children look on command, and repeat directions. Draw pictures of the directions so that a child who finds it difficult to follow directions has a focus for his/her attention. Remember to social praise children's understanding of the directions.

2. *Talking is always good for someone.* However, it also can be a block to listening and understanding. Praise all children who are listening. Give the talkers incentive to listen rather than to draw their attention and others' attention to their talking. Know their interests and ask them to talk to you afterwards about them but meanwhile ask them to focus on what you have to say. You realize that their ability to look to direction and task is hard. So after a short introduction, (before their talk) give a particular task or attention for those who find it hard. Give the talkers a special time to talk to each other at the end of the listening session. Find a focus as above to retain attention and be ready to praise.

3. *Fidgeting is not a problem for all children* but it is indicative of children who find the classroom structure hard to work in. Children who fidget need to have some breaks. You need to not draw attention to the difficulty but provide the child with meaningful activity as an option whilst others manage a longer task or listening period. Make sure that as the fidgeting decreases, your expectation must be greater. (See longer programming.)

4. *Calling out is always a problem* and most teachers will respond too late. Unfortunately children like this have trained the teacher to respond angrily because the damage has been done. And how can the teacher ask another question without the same thing happening? Which children call out? Are the answers usually correct or incorrect? Suggest the 'caller' leave the group with two other children and to quietly explain the answers to them. Teacher can repeat questions for those remaining. Reward all the children who did not call out. Be ready for the situation and use the time to train children to turn take and share in game situations. Start by asking questions personal and individual to each child so that everyone gets praised for answering questions. Get the children to think up and ask the questions of each other.

5. *Not attending to task,* for whatever reason the child has, may also be the teacher's problem. Did the child understand the task set and is it one they can manage with their particular capability? Ask the child if they have everything before the task starts. Praise the child every few minutes as to standard of task, attention to task, or all group praise for attention to task.

6. *Telling tales on other children* is about one child's own lack of self aware-ness. Ignore tales unfounded and ask the child direct questions about his or her own involvements. Work on child's play and involvement with other children in the room. Praise the child and all the children using good social comments and further suggestions for interaction. It is always good to 'include' a child in praise with the group as well as individually.

7. *A bully* should be the focus of the teacher's concerns as much as the receiver of the bullying. The bully has often experienced the bullying and the effect of intervention should be to promote good social relationships and to help the bully focus on his own difficulties in relating to other children. Remove children from situation, but place them together safely to discuss better ways of managing whatever difficulty they may be having. You might even take part in the discussion to model ways of negotiating.

8. *A child out of seat* does not necessarily mean that the child is not learning to potential. However, it does mean that it disrupts other children or holds up the progress of the teacher within a lesson. The child may only manage a certain time in seat but needs to have a focus other than in seat within the class where s/he might go for several minutes before returning to seat. The child could have a project on desk that can be completed as an incentive to stay in seat for the chosen number of minutes. Praise in-seat behaviour. Consider activities that you have prepared that engross the child enough to stay in seat for that period of time. Engineer the situation so that you can praise.

9. *Annoying other children* can mean many things from prodding, shouting at, banging desks, amongst many others. Children who annoy others often have a multi-problematic behavioural structure and any of the above should be thought as usable in this case. These children may need a responsibility that gives them position amongst their peers. They may need help to know other ways that you like children to ask for attention. If the child has a low self esteem, then finding strengths s/he has would be an advantage.

10. *Destroying their own work and/or that of others* suggests that a child needs to have short tasks and be removed by the teacher, with praise and given another task with a time rather than a completion requirement. When others complete work, teacher should move to child and to give language to the child in the form of praise and look appropriately at completed work. Some people note that children's behaviour may worsen after praise. Children

unused to praise are unsure how to react and need to be helped through the stage of acceptance. Rather than to stop praise, a teacher should continue until the child can receive, react and be motivated by the verbal attention.

11. *Children have ways of combatting anxieties and lack of confidence* in being able to approach others for play or talk. Adults may see this and try to befriend the child. Often this does not help the child's sociability *Circle Time* (Murray White, 1996) is a useful way to help such children. Adults can encourage all children to share tips with each other about what to play and share. Raising confidence and self esteem can be important here.

12. *The issue here is not to lengthen attention span.* Teacher sometimes feels that this must be possible and child and adult end up with a feeling of disappointment. Much better is to look at how best to use those short attention spans, so that the child learns maximally and finishes work in the time s/he can manage. It is important to improve a child's motivation to do well and continue onto the next thing.

13. *Any way, it is wrong to steal.* Collectively dealing with what is right or wrong, sets the boundaries. A child who steals needs a new focus. This may not be solved simply for some children so it is best to see it in terms of managing the child away from acquiring, giving the opportunity but not the access and working on the strengths of the child.

14. *Children like to repeat tasks they can do.* It boosts confidence and makes them feel successful. The fear of failure and the idea that tasks may be 'too hard' is strong in some children. These children need to build their information slower than others. Children develop in different ways. Their ability to learn and their confidence to learn may mean that the teacher may not only have to differentiate but also to consider how much a child is ready to take on. The problem may be rare in a class but the child's behaviour will be apparent.

What an adult must always remember is that every child, every teacher in every situation are all using behaviour to solve some kinds of problems and the best way to solve them is to merge and manipulate the behaviours so that there will be a positive outcome. It is not always easy and for people who see difficult behaviours rarely, the opportunity to think openly with flexibility is a frightening obstacle. Quite often the response is that if the child will not respond immediately to long-term praise, smiley faces and shouting, then nothing else seems possible but exclusion. The teacher then says that s/he has tried everything but the child is unresponsive. There is then a long list of the child's misdemeanours listed and the impossibilities of success. Clearly a teacher cannot be all things to all children but a more diagnostic approach with remediating ideas will often take the stress out of a whole classroom approach. Teachers should also be sympathetic and understand that programmes often make a problem worse before it improves and that their colleagues who are working to solve a problem will have to work through this period however impractical it may look. In this way teachers can then be supportive of each other and each other's plans.

Practical Use of Behavioural Therapies in the Classroom

Now that we have examined in some detail the possible practical strategies to use in the classroom for more transient behaviours, we will go on to look at how such practical ways of managing behaviour fit in with particular therapies. The use of the word therapies in this instance is to take its broadest form of ways in which acquisition of good learning and social behaviours can come about by applying a range of psychological and managerial approaches. All teachers can apply all of the following suggested therapies with thought, creativity and consistency. There may be some that teachers have not thought about in the context of classroom management of individuals as well as groups. Similarly, some will require more attention to detail than others and some will be easier to apply with greater effect over time. The following comments are suggestions for use and discussion in order to focus attention on ways in which children are managed and creative ways in which to manage children. Reference will be made to the ways in which each therapy can be used in special and mainstream settings.

A Token Economy System

Twenty-four Hour Token Economy System in a Special School

Rationalization   Is useful for children who exhibit a range of behavioural and emotional difficulties. It provides an environment which is consistent, stable, positive and which encourages balanced appropriate social responses in all situations throughout the day.

   The structure is strong and has easily attainable objectives through the day that encourages success. It is a system which mirrors our social system of earning and spending on things necessary or desired. Value is placed on activities and objects which in turn give meaning to learning appropriate behaviours. It is a system that works over twenty-four hours and gives continuity and equality to all the school day ensuring that the children's time is used positively and allowing both teachers and care staff to operate within one system.

   A Token System is a sound theory suited to a school environment of twenty-four hour control and management. However, the system can be modified to suit a day school. It is a system in which all staff can work together towards agreed goals for behaviour. Tokens are awarded for children co-operating in basic social situations. In this way there are expectations for mealtimes, playtimes, assembly and residential times.

A Token System becomes part of the children's environment. Advertising, discussion, earning and spending all give the children a sense of value and independence. It must be instantly recognized that, because this is a positive system, social rewards are then built in. Adults are able to give children a great amount of encouragement and emotional support without the onus of a 'negative punishment' situation. Its best feature is that a child may have a problem in a short space of time, but be encouraged to move onto the next token. Looking ahead to the good time stops the child and adult from continuing the problem and helps the child to learn to control her/himself and to get back on a positive course.

Targeting behaviour   Appropriate behaviour means more time to spend on acquiring better educative behaviour. In addition to this, appropriate behaviour means a better social atmosphere where children can develop good relationships. More particular and individual behavioural needs are reached by targeting individuals and groups. Each child is seen as an individual with their own set of goals according to their own stage of development and independence. Communicating the targets to all adults means that adults are consistent in their approach to each individual child and in helping them to achieve their targets with individual needs and with individual programmes. With the security of the token system, targeting individuals means that the child develops a conscious level of his or her own needs. It develops a language for the child that helps him internalize his/her difficulties and find ways to deal with them. Instead of the child being inconsistently handled by each adult and increasing the child's manipulation of adults, the child is able to form more consistent relationships.

The individual targets and group expectations form the basis for the token rewards. However, the child is required to be pro-active within this process and for this reason children and staff are encouraged to discuss targets, rewards and strategies. Here again, the use of a common language facilitates the process.

Delivery of tokens   When a child receives a token s/he knows that s/he has achieved the adult expectations set within a limited time, usually ten to fifteen minutes. In this way the child receives social praise and encouragement which is the basis to learning and gives the child the chance to recognize his own success.

If the child has not conformed to expectations, he does not receive the token but may work towards receiving the next. In this way it provides a framework that emphasizes the acquisition of appropriate skills and strategies.

'Bum bags' can be used to hold tokens for adults and children alike and the child knows that they are to do with the giving and receiving of tokens. Bum bags can form part of a uniform. This gives the children a sense of belonging and the responsibility for caring for their own tokens. Some children may even wear them to bed.

Collection and spending of tokens   In an exemplary system, children can get up to 75 tokens over a twenty-four hour time period. The day can be divided into time periods with a specified number of tokens for each period. Children are made aware of what behaviours are acceptable and would thus earn a certain number of tokens. The end of each twenty-four hour period can be at 3.45 p.m. At this time the child may visit a school shop to spend these tokens on activities, toys, books or savers. With the exception of the savers, the tokens should be spent daily.

Sharing the system   The system can always be shared. Parents may be invited to use it at home so that the method can be used to its fullest potential. This is a definite way for parents to work with children although they must be aware of all the many factors. They should spend time observing and discussing strategies and approaches through the token economy system. There are over one hundred different aspects and uses of the system.

One particular school (see acknowledgments) had a short ten minute brain storming session and came up with the following elements that characterized its system.

Reflecting on aspects of a token economy system in a special school

1   The whole system is based on positive reinforcement.
2   The child has immediate reward for appropriate behaviour.
3   The child has the opportunity to stop and change his or her behaviour continually.
4   The child is active in developing appropriate social behaviours.
5   The adult is actively involved in the whole process of developing appropriate behaviours.
6   Anything that is earned cannot be taken away.
7   If you haven't got a bumbag, you can't earn tokens.
8   Deliberate loss of playground equipment is charged.
9   But there is a 'creative' charging system linking behaviour to a charge e.g. spitting is for Dettol to clean it up.
10 When a child throws tokens, he or she is given the opportunity to retrieve these tokens. The period of time allowed for this is up to one session or one hour.
11 The adult will effectively organize the best periods of time to reward with tokens when out on activity.
12 Adult taking the child to the doctors/buying clothes gives out tokens according to specific day time rates.
13 Residential area keeps tokens one per child per day for on-going target related to residential aspects. This gives a possibility of one giant* at the end of the week.
14 Doing tasks extra well does not mean extra tokens.
15 Targets can be linked to token acquisition in particular circumstances.
16 Continual negotiation is open for developing aspects of the Token Economy System.

17   Tokens are based on the quality of the behaviour and not the task in hand which is an educational issue.

18   Clarification between who gives out the tokens in the classroom is between individual teachers and assistants.

19   The question is raised is the token or the social praise the greater reinforcer? Or is it a combination of the two?

20   It is an expectation that all children will have a green and yellow voucher*.

21   If a voucher is torn, the child will be given an opportunity to stick it together.

22   The child has to be in the right place at the right time in order to score.

23   Tokens are only received and put into bumbags.

24   The child's behaviour often has to be managed to help the child earn the token.

25   Good things must be said to children for them to earn and jointly learn positive qualities of social behaviour.

26   The token structure maintains a reasonable expectation for all children through the twenty-four hours.

27   The Token Economy System is only part of the process of managing behaviour.

28   Adults talking about behaviour and tokens model communication about what is important to the children.

29   Children must see the giving of tokens as fair.

30   Why tokens are given should be clear to all members of the group.

31   When a child receives a low score at the end of the day, it means that he has had some good times during the day.

32   The daily graph gives the child a feeling for the process of his or her own behaviour.

33   If a child is earning none or little, then the adult should look at their own behaviour, at what he or she is not doing.

34   Children are always amazed at the way staff in the day know what his or her behaviour has been in the night time. If the staff have not caught up then the number of giants is a good indication of the child's behaviour.

35   The Token Economy System works for everybody.

36   Key workers and teachers focus on children every three weeks to talk over progress problems and plans.

* Five yellow tokens equal one giant. Five giants make a big green saver. The yellow giant voucher is to record number of night-time giants and the green voucher is to record a total of yellow voucher and day time tokens. Seven giants are possible over night and eight giants are possible during the day.

The future   The token economy system can grow with any school's development and the changing needs of the children. The system reflects the greater society and therefore is easy for the children to recognize their position with it. Children can easily adapt to new systems once their behaviour has stabilized.

A Token Economy System in a Mainstream School

The equivalent system in a mainstream classroom would follow the principles as set out above; the most important being, that whatever the group or individual had earned throughout the day or period must be 'spent' at the end of the designated period and certainly by the end of the day. The accumulation of points or ticks, bottle tops, match sticks must be tradable and the rewards must be visible and right to the individual or group. Short term token systems can be effective in mainstream classes and can be tailored to solve particular problems over periods of time. The idea of a 'good time' lesson toward the end of the week, may have activities that the children can earn either as small groups or as individuals.

'Special' rewards designated by the adult can be important motivators. An adult should work on making the rewards desirable before the system can begin.

> I knew a father who designated a high shelf his 'special' toy shelf. In themselves the toys were not valuable but in the way in which they were handled and respected by the adult, they came to be desired by the child. The toys had even greater value because the father shared his time and toys when they were taken off the shelf.

Value in some instances must be taught and is crucial in the planning of strategic programmes.

Social Milieu

In a Special School

Creating opportunities for group co-operation and independence are paramount aims for children with special needs in particular. This is accomplished by maximizing individual participation at whatever levels possible. The aim is to present the child with opportunities which will develop social skills in relation to group operation.

In a Mainstream School

The integrated day itself provides the opportunity for children to move appropriately and independently from on situation or activity to another. Principles behind the progression of activities from the child's point of view should be that the completion of one task is motivated by the attraction of the task to come, as well as the need to operate in the awareness of the needs of the group without sacrificing those of the individual. Opportunities to create situations are best shared. Schools that recognize the need to train learning behaviour and skills will encourage staff to work together. Periods spent might range from a morning thirty minute session to the use of a playtime.

Modelling

In a Special School

In the lives of many children there is little positive adult interaction. In my experience I find that in many cases parental involvement may include the well meaning providing of materials and toys at home but not the participation. In others, there is a dependence on media entertainment. For the children the consequences of this are a lack of development in social skills, as well as language, intrinsic motivation and in learning behaviours. The ability to form relationships is also limited. The active adult is important in helping such children. I find that the strategy of modelling behaviour helps to increase teachers' confidence in personal change and development. It also promotes involvement with children and a more active participation in developing ideas about how the children are taught. In consistent observations I have made, children quickly pick up the teacher's involvement in the tasks and attention to tasks over time does improve.

In a Mainstream School

The teacher can emulate good adult-child and child-child relationships through modelling in a variety of learning situations. Good examples would be in the teaching of play skills for games in the classroom as well as on the playground. Much recent interest has centred around the need for staff to be active during playtimes in the teaching as well as the modelling of games which promote co-operation. When volunteers or classroom assistants are available, modelling of positive social relationships and shared activities are examples for the children. Talking about children who are presenting good listening or sitting skills encourages off-task children to copy them.

In a less formal way it is always a good idea to give the children the opportunity to see how the teacher can sit and read silently or model with plasticine or arrange the pieces to prepare a jigsaw. The scope is endless in the every day management of a classroom and can become common practice rather than a forced therapy, over time.

Body Language

In a Special School

Staff are likely to be skilled in the art of being close to children in ways which emphasize going towards them both physically and emotionally rather than away from them. Teachers who walk slowly around the room, help the children to settle. A frenzied or anxious teacher sets the scene in the classroom for a too busy teacher to talk and listen.

In a Mainstream School

Likely approaches are the teacher's use of voice; perfecting the art of being able to use a range from loud to soft appropriate to the situation. When used consistently the class will pick up the 'hidden messages' and thus enable the teacher to project meaning and expectation without becoming verbally negative. Always try to walk slowly to a problem, to keep moving throughout activities and not to sit stuck to the desk, all of which will give mixed messages to children who will be very acute at assessing the teacher's attitudes towards them. Of great importance is the use of eye-contact, both as a means of class and group control at times when children may perceive that they are unobserved. Most teachers are so busy organizing that they forget that each child is waiting for that particular eye contact. Getting children to answer questions, means that hands go up, children are chosen and they need to get the message with personal eye-contact that they have the floor. A perfect example of a harassed approach, is the teacher who wants the more theoretical side to be over so that peace can reign with the busy work. S/he forgets to wait for quiet, so that when a child is called on they have to wait while the teacher explains to the other children the need to listen to the answer, by the time this may or may not have been achieved, the chosen child has either forgotten, doesn't care or has joined the giggling. Body language from the teacher must initially say that this is an important time of the day.

Cognitive Talk

In a Special School

For children with poor language abilities particular emphasis will be placed on the need to give the child or class the language in which to express feelings and behaviours. This therapy facilitates the teacher and children's ability to use a common cognitive framework in which to conduct activity in the classroom and thus facilitate understanding rather than frustration. Talk is important for memory. Memory is about our experiences and we all use the knowledge of our experiences as the basis for planning our lives, either the next ten minutes or the next ten years.

In a Mainstream School

Teachers might consider the ways in which they manage to give the child the opportunity to focus on their behaviour as being important through their language. This applies equally to behaviour towards one another and between teacher and pupil. To assume an unreasonably high level of cognitive functioning will inevitably lead to conflict when a child is presented with solutions or sanctions that are misunderstood. Do not underestimate the need to restructure and develop cognitive skills, in particular language at all levels of schooling. A useful tip is for the teacher to always consider themself to be a language teacher as well as valuing other specialisms. When possible give pictorial clues or physical prompts. Some children may not be piecing together everything you have said and will need to relate what is said to something more concrete. Showing as one talks is effective because behaviour is better if attention is focused.

Peer Group Control

In a Special School

Not successfully used as a therapy because of wide ranges in abilities and difficulties. If used as positive statement, peer control can be effective. An example might be, 'Everyone has tried hard and I am pleased with you all'. If there are a number of children to control, and the teacher asks the others to help the offenders to manage, the result is never positive.

In a Mainstream School

This type of therapy can be used successfully when used in short bursts with definable behaviours. It can be a bad thing when the control is negative and when the group is encouraging and rewarding the wrong thing. In an attempt to manage a class this way the short-term result will be chaos at best and no long-term results can be described as working towards either control or management. It is a tempting approach to use but children are not always subject to the social forces for which we give them credit. Therefore, be careful and ensure that it is used sensibly.

The group will need help to know that they are strong in their positive behaviours and not in the negative behaviour. Consider the benefits from placing a disruptive child in a better behaved group. Never isolate a table of children with poor behaviour self management.

Flooding

In a Special School

The opportunity to rehearse the undesirable behaviour to the point of doing it at a time that would become undesirable and over-important in context is possible in special school settings where there is more opportunity to work on individual programmes, sometimes requiring one-to-one intervention. An example might be the possibility of a child to throw the offending chair repeatedly on a field or to make animal noises even louder and for longer in a corridor away from others. The consequence must be sufficiently negative, undesirable and above all contingent on the undesirable behaviour itself.

In a Mainstream School

There exists the possibility that the behaviour could escalate if this therapy is used unsuccessfully and therefore the behaviours for which it can succeed have to be looked at carefully. The child who is always sharpening his/her pencil may tire of the strategy if required to sharpen all pencils at a time which is undesirable. It is always important to keep in mind exactly what behaviour is being reinforced.

Aversion

In a Special School

Aversion therapy is not often used and then it must be used carefully, written up, recorded and discussed. In a simpler form, garlic in chocolate bars has been used to stop petty pilfering in school.

In a Mainstream School

A practical response to a class which is initially out of hand might be to put everything in cupboards when equipment is badly treated and give the children the right to earn the things back in the classroom according to strict procedures as controlled by the teacher. In general this therapy should be last on the list for use with individual children.

Extrinsic and Intrinsic Rewards

In a Special School

In special schools, extrinsic rewards are most commonplace. The aim is to reduce extrinsic rewards in order to encourage children's development of intrinsic rewards. Children will show this development by their behaviour. Children who feel intrinsically rewarded can show that they are taking pleasure in completing work and can plan what they would like to do. Extrinsic rewards can be either tangible or intangible. It is important to control and manage extrinsic rewarding in order for it to be effective.

In a Mainstream School

It must be the ultimate aim for all teachers to develop in children the drive, motivation and satisfaction that can be generated from within themselves, for themselves. This is very difficult to measure and will need to be trained up and developed just like any other behaviour. Children will develop intrinsic appreciation over time with carefully used extrinsic rewards. Children receive a great deal of pleasure from knowing that they are doing well and will reward the adult by staying within the boundaries. The 'good work sticker' will become redundant when the child perceives the success as being something that is felt rather than public recognition. The child will not necessarily recognize the worth of intrinsic outcomes without the necessary language and thought process and the teacher will need to make explicit feelings of pride, pleasure or satisfaction. Consider the importance of encouraging the child to smile to show that s/he is pleased with the task that has just been completed.

Sociable and Tangible Rewards

In a Special School

Intangible and tangible rewards have been proved to be very potent in the education of special school children. The need to reinforce appropriate behaviours with rewards that might at first appear to be 'over the top' are very effective. Children are always motivated by food as well as things which would appear of little value to adults. Some children have to be trained to recognize a reward. To do this, an adult has to place the child in a situation in which the child is doing the right thing for however small a time, and then expressing by word, positive physical prompt, (thumbs up, quick hug, big smiles, good words) and the use of a sensory or edible reward. The obvious process then goes to rewarding when the child responds appropriately independently and then to generalizing the behaviour spontaneously. Rewarding tangibly should always be accompanied by language (sign, verbal). Rewards initially can range from single Smarties to the use of objects and to privileges of any kind. The range is infinite depending on child and circumstance.

Social rewarding is always acceptable by most children. For some being rewarded socially however has not been practised in the past and these children will appear to respond negatively initially. Some adults will give up after this reaction saying that the child's behaviour worsens on reward. Perseverance however will show an improved acceptance and eventual pleasure from the child.

In a Mainstream School

The availability of an adult's time is often a good social reward especially in a large class. A period of independent working or responsibility can eventually also be seen as a social reward leading toward that intrinsic reward. The monitor system can be used to great effect with all children and need not be seen as a privilege, unattainable by most. Making rewards within the classroom is a matter of management. A craft table with choice, a special drink area and biscuits with quiet reading, a play area to use with a chosen friend, games boards, taking messages, decorating a classroom board, the list can be endless but must be used within the long-term strategies for the class. For instance, the stickers for good work, or smiley faces for managing play should accumulate to earn an activity which might practise some of the skills taken to acquire the smiley faces and stickers. Preparation before school starts in planning management procedures with projected ideas would help the year once the class intake is known.

Whole class rewards could be reading the favourite books, a walk to find something interesting outside, inviting another class into the hall to share a short video with drinks, games session with favourite games, music tape during craft. Teachers can find any number of solutions to rewards. Teachers are always busy and therefore just looking at a child and talking can be rewarding.

Sometimes rewards, used incorrectly can cause a negative behaviour to continue. Look at the following combinations in Figure 2.1, probably familiar, but worth reiterating. There are only two instances in which a response can be seen to be having a positive effect. Which are they?

Further Strategies and Therapies

Other therapies and methods worthy of consideration include:

Assertive Discipline

Assertive discipline has a popular following at present. The principle is for the adult to manage to the rule and for children to work within and understand a firm consistent programme. It probably works best in a secondary setting although some primary schools may disagree.

Figure 2.1:   *Reinforcement of appropriate and inappropriate behaviour*

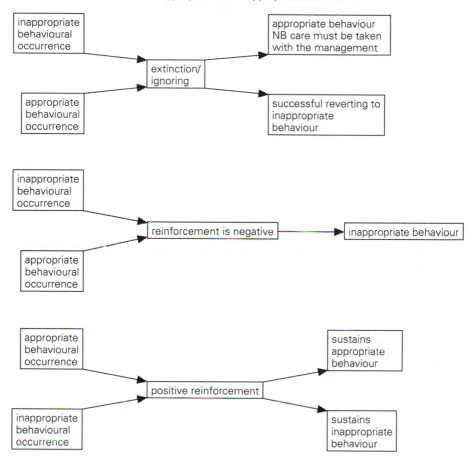

Individual Programming

This is a system that works continually in special school settings, where a lot of consideration and individual scheduling may have to take place. Here also includes the important issue of certain children with difficulties having one-one relationship within a mainstream setting. The teacher must realize the dangers as well as the positive aspects of this. The adult must be able to give independence to the child in the programme rather than to take it away which is what happens in the main.

Backward and Forward Chaining

Sometimes a complete task may appear very daunting to a child. He or she may have to start near the end of a task and achieve success before learning the next stage. An example of this might be tying shoe laces. Tightening the bow and feeling the excitement of completion may be motivating enough to try standing up the bows next.

Contracting

A child may like to see how her or his individual programme works and to take part in how it develops. Contracting sets up a programme between adult and child and both sign an understanding of it. It works best however, if again the adult actively pursues the development rather than creating and leaving it to continue like magic in the hands of the child.

Fitting into the Eco-system

Working out how the environment can be adapted to the needs of the individuals within it depends on a teacher's long term development plans and should include differentiated work and resources to include both behavioural and academic differences. Eco-systems are about balance. In any habitat, when one factor changes, others change to accommodate it. Teacher behaviour cannot change without it making a difference to the classroom and its inhabitants. Looking to develop new behaviours in one child means that other factors have to be managed that will be affected by the new programme. It is important to look at new ways of dealing with problematic behaviours and manipulating situations so that behaviours can be managed. The ecosystemic approach is based on particular set of understandings of the ways in which individual's behaviour is related to (i) his or her particular way of seeing the world, and (ii) the interactions he or she has with the other people in his or her life. Classrooms as ecosystems can be explored in other literature by such people as Paul Cooper (1992).

Box 4: Continued story

What next? 'Start as you mean to go on' is always an excellent phrase. As is also 'be prepared'. It is also good to remember that the first twenty minutes of the day are best in terms of attention. I decided that these pointers could come in useful. I therefore assumed that all the children did not recognise phonics. I assumed that no child could take and carry out directions. I took it that no child could stay on a task for longer than ten minutes. All the children were healthy, they could all learn to have a group coherence, they could all learn. Armed with the basics in my mind, I planned out the first day very carefully.

　　How does one start to manage? I organized the tables around me in a semi circle and placed a chair if I needed it in the middle. I was going to use simple commands and I was going to repeat them until the child/ren complied. I would speak firmly and positively. I had books

---

made individually and a simple task of sounds related to the SRA phonic attack. I had a small box of the favourite Smarties in my pocket.

What decisions do you make about what strategies to use? Why Smarties? At that time there was no token system in this day school and I had to reward quickly and consistently in order to concentrate the children on positively learning that which was totally in conflict with their last term's attitude and behaviour. I had had no training in systems or management and my methods were all new to me. It was my first attempt at controlling and managing teenage, maladjusted and aggressive children.

How do you make children respect a room and environment that has meant very little? You make the room mean something important by using words and modelling interest in detail. You use the word 'our' room. You discuss with the children how it will grow. You make it clear to start for maximum attention. You fill it slowly with work completed by children who have not completed before.

Where do you start teaching and what to teach? You must start where the children are and you make sure that they understand one stage before careering off to another. It is good to use the National Curriculum but not at the expense of good teaching. You gain attention and make sure children listen and you use language that they understand and you check that they do understand. Start simple, and the classroom can grow as the children manage. Special items can be introduced that build the identity of the group.

No-one told me I would be faced with this in teacher training. I made a good group of children in this classroom but had I known what to do I may not have had the anxieties I experienced in setting this up and other initiatives in the school. In a sense I had to experiment in the classroom which paid off in this example but might have been disastrous in another. These were my early days when management of children was not as popular as today.

Conclusion

As we have worked through some of these strategies and therapies it should be possible to see that they are all fairly straight forward and logical in application. Also that a combination of several may be effective. It is important to know the dynamics of the individuals and groups in order to apply the strategies with confidence and to be able to choose the one that looks as if it will work best. The information above is not extensive and therefore should interest be aroused then further investigations at the library are suggested. Books and articles that may be appropriate are included in the bibliography. They can all be traced through the local library. You should also explore the journal sections; most articles include useful bibliography.

3 Observation Techniques and a Discussion on Perception

Introduction

Observing, looking, perceiving, scanning, watching all these words seem to imply very different ways of seeing. We do seem to choose them all quite specifically. Observing implies a planned distance with intent. Looking has always meant for me a perusal, in hopes of finding. Perceiving is more personal and is about bringing something of your own to a situation. Scanning is an overall looking and watching is more about how we explain what we are doing. Clearly these are my own semantics, you may have different ideas. The difference in what we see and say we can see depends on why we are looking and how we record what we are seeing and what we are looking at. We can either be informed about what we are watching or we are looking for information. I may look at a flight of birds. Someone else may see it as a particular flight of particular birds. Someone else may be observing a particular aspect of the flight implying a much deeper understanding of the flight than my looking. Teachers must do more than watch a class of children. Teachers need to see all the children as particular, the way in which the class works together and be able to pick out particular aspects.

What is Observation?

Why do we observe in the first place? After all we are looking at activities and things all day. What makes observing different from just looking? The answer is that it is meaningful and by observing we are trying to make sense of what we see and gain clues as to what to do about what we see. We are looking, but more deeply and learning is an important outcome.

We can learn from observing others because looking purposefully at others can provide information as to what kinds of behaviour lead to which consequences or what antecedents lead to what behaviours. Looking is a very strong tool, when a child is not being watched, s/he feels ignored.

We are watching other people's behaviour all the time and the action of observation is very complex. That complexity has to do with what we are learning from the experience. Because we all have different levels of tolerance and social expectations, we have to be very clear what we are wanting to observe and why. We also have a varying understanding of appropriate and inappropriate behaviours. What we like and what we do not like can best be exemplified by our reactions to various paintings. Our responses will be varied but equally valid.

Making a record of what we see as objectively as possible, means that we can share our observations and compare our perceptions of the incidents, an example of the observation of an individual child is cited later in the chapter.

When Should Teachers Decide to Make Observations?

Most teachers feel that they are observing all day, but for the most part a teacher is scanning. Because of this it is the most obviously obtrusive behaviours that receive most attention. In this way, a teacher is quick to pick up on a potential problem. However, the extent of the on-going problem is probably not so obvious. Particular children may be presenting behaviours that go unnoticed but lead up towards inappropriate learning behaviour in the long term. Scanning is the way teachers manage because they are busy people. However, sometimes it is necessary to be more deeply involved and committed to observing in order to learn something about a child's or class of children's particular behaviour.

In order to observe and record what you are looking at you need to be objective. Remember:

- Subjective reporting has a place but it is not useful in being able to give information to somebody else who needs to act on it. Subjective also tends to be emotive and has a gossip factor. We are more subjective when we are talking about ourselves and our viewpoints.
- Objective reporting however is rather like a police report in that it concentrates on facts and the order of events. Objectivity has to do with collecting information that can be used more generally and acted upon. Being objective in the classroom helps a teacher to be fair.

What is Perception?

Perception involves an interpretation of the sense data provided by the stimulus/ child or group; the observer's past experience, motivational state and expectations influence the meaning of the observed behaviour and in turn help determine the observer's response. Therefore, our perceptions will be coloured by our own experiences. We all carry our own suitcase of our past with us to new experiences. When you are reporting what you have seen, your perception can be mediated by having a process that will guide your observations. This is when you focus on a problem, record a baseline, set a programme, record, reflect, modify and so on. More formal observations will be included later in this chapter.

Utilising perception is important because although it can be subjective, it can also shed light on a more general picture of a child around school. Formal observations cannot always be made and collecting information verbally from all adults may help share a child who has problems.

I am always surprised when I share information to find just how differently behaviours are viewed by others than by myself. Not only do we have varied perceptions but also various levels of tolerance. Because of this, how we report to others is coloured by our understanding of appropriate behaviour. Another factor is the behaviour of the child in relation to previous behaviours and information that we might carry that begs the statement, 'for him/her that is excellent'. If you haven't got access to prior information, then you would only have present behaviour to go on and you may not feel it is excellent at all. In which case you may be at odds with another adult in discussing what you feel is acceptable and what is not. In discussing a child, I once remarked how well he was doing on a particular day. A lunch time carer walked in and said that as far as she was concerned this was not true. She had just had to hold him for ten minutes so that he wouldn't go after and hurt another child. As it happened, the problem was only ten minutes but in that time the carer had been hurt. As I had not observed this behaviour, the information modified my initial opinion. I might continue to believe that in my terms ten minutes out of a day in which a child was normally out of control ten to twelve times, was encouraging. The carer may feel that the problem has clouded any positive feelings she might have for the child at that time and her perception of his day. However, what I said may have modified her conclusions about the child's day. This is good practice also for the discussion of behaviour with groups of children who may have similar misconceptions about their behaviour that day.

In looking for an intervention for a very difficult child, it may be best to look at a much fuller picture of him or her from a variety of perceptions. The following sheets are examples of a simple format you might like to follow in a process of setting up a more general programme. The formulation sheet (1) gets together the information very simply in order to get ideas for intervention. The second sheet sets up the intervention schedule (2) that is possible for all. A programme that is too demanding asks for failure. Just as important is a separate sheet called 'My special behaviour chart', with the child's name, what he or she is expected to contribute and where help will come from (not included).

Processing Our Observations

A common way of giving structure and meaning to what you observe is to remember the ABC; Antecedent, Behaviour and Consequences. An Antecedent is everything that you saw happening before a behaviour. Behaviour is the isolated action that you can see. The Consequence is what happens next. Although we often think that knowing the antecedent, behaviour and consequence will help in setting up a programme for behaviour for the child, I

Intervention Formulation Sheet

Name of child *Andy Smith*	**Intervention Schedule**
Adults involved	**Who and how**
B. Grady (teacher) H. Miles (TA) D. Long (Deputy Head) M. Hove (Midday Assistant)	*B. Grady*
Observations and perceptions of adults	*To be aware of activities of small group and be ready to reward Andy when he responds well in large group*
Andy is always trying to get my attention. He is loud and answers questions before anyone else.	
Strengths — He can be helpful with children who do have learning difficulties.	*To be aware that it will take a term or more to make differences*
B. Grady	
	H. Miles
If I take Andy away to work with he is fine. He likes working with one adult. I usually take him when the teacher has group work to do.	*To learn how to run a small group in training up speaking and listening skills. To remove the group twice a week for ten minutes.*
H. Miles	
	D. Long
Andy is impossible at lunch time. He is noisy and he teases other children. If they tell him to stop or call for me, he kicks them before he was off.	*To make time with Andy positive, desireable and constructive.*
Strengths — He can be good with the younger children	*M. Hove*
M. Hove	*To encourage Andy to join the play skills group for ten minutes each lunch time*

Adult expectations	**Child's name**
I would like him to listen in group time	*Andy Smith*
B. Grady	**Monday** *withdrawal by H. Miles*
I would like to see him helping in class instead of coming out with me. I can't be available for other children H. Miles	**Tuesday** *withdrawal by H. Miles*
	Wednesday *Participate in large group*
I would like to see him playing football with the other bogs M. Hove	*Each lunch time — Ten minutes formal play*
I would like to see less of him in my room D. Long	**Child's Name**
Ideas for intervention	
Assistant to take out four or five children to do listening and speaking exercises to include Andy. The group to work on a reward basis.	**What we are going to do together**
When Andy practices skills in larger group, he is verbally rewarded by teacher.	**What teacher says**
Andy only goes to Deputy's room when he has done well and not when he has not done well.	**What child says**
Teacher to spend ten minutes of each lunch time with Andy and several other children building up playing skills.	**Long term aim**
	Have we made it?

also like to think of it as a chart for looking at the adult behaviour. What was planned, what did you do and what were the consequences? Examples are given below of *Incident Forms*. They are about one incident but reported from two different points of view. Take some time to think about which one is giving you the information that will help you to know best what has happened. In this case it is two children and not the adults!

A	B
Incident Report Form	Incident Report Form
Children involved — David and Ben	Children involved — David and Ben
Day: Monday Date: 1996–7 Time: 10.30	Day: Monday Date: 1996–97 Time: 10.30
Location: Playground Activity: Hide'n Seek	Location: Playground Activity: Hide'n Seek
A. Antecedents (note anything before B) *David was looking for children and went further into the bushes toward a large tree.*	A. Antecedents (note anything before B) *We were all playing Hide'n Seek and David was enjoying being the 'seeker'. He likes all the children although he is wary of Ben. I think Ben had it in his head to do something — and I think David was looking for a problem.*
B. Behaviour *1. Ben came from behind the tree* *2. Ben was waving a stick* *3. David moved toward him* *4. The stick hit David across the head* *5. David fell to floor* *6. Ben dropped the stick and ran away*	B. Behaviour *I could imagine that David probably said something when he was close to Ben which again probably made Ben angry. Ben wanted to really hurt David and looked for a stick. So, as David approached, he was ready for him. He thought how to do the most damage and brought the stick down onto the unsuspecting David. David was really hurt and I got the feeling that Ben was secretly pleased and ran away.*
C. Consequences *1. Ben did not earn the token for play-time* *2. Ben was asked to say what had happened and apologise to David* *3. Ben to hold adult's hand for the next three play sessions to help him to think about co-operation.*	C. Consequences *David taken to the medical room in the end. Although he said nothing, I think Ben was sorry when he saw what he had done.*
Medical attention *David to medical room; ice pack, antiseptic cream*	Medical Attention *ice pack, antiseptic cream*

Writing incident forms is a good way of keeping a record of children's behaviour. Reportage is important, however, so is the information that it holds. It should help to give clues about the timing of interventions.

You may need to find out about an individual and his/her behaviour in a variety of learning situations in order to compare adaptations. For this you will clearly need other adults to help in the observations. In the classroom, having another observer is usually better than having to manage the more complex observations during teaching time.

General Individual Observation (M)

This particular observation was of an individual child and it was necessary to find out how much he was responding to in-class activities. Teachers needing to get a general picture like this, will need an observer to record within a set framework. The observer doesn't tick boxes, s/he writes what s/he sees as objectively as possible.

M Heavily Supervised on a One-to-one Basis

- behaviour is manageable
- still very easily distracted, especially by others' behaviour
- brought back to attention by 'listen to me' and 'look at me'
- ready to begin again when full attention and when quiet and calm
  N.B. important to bring him back so that the problem does not escalate
  Question — M will sit quietly, is this because he can do it or because he has close supervision and is responding to that?
- does ask questions 'what here?'/'what are they?'
  N.B. M asks questions but does not enter into conversation
- slow but will get there — if he has a problem with work it is important to re-present the work, especially with maths

M on His Own

- very difficult to work on his own
- manifests itself in fidgeting, chatting, active looking around — will return to work only for short periods, distraction then continues
- very difficult working on own
  N.B. needs supervision if only intermittently, for example: 'are you using that properly?'
  N.B. likes to be playing, using something
  N.B. hands on ear when hearing noise
  N.B. noisy when changing activities (adults ignore the noise, try to get his attention)
  N.B. better to say things to develop behaviours with Martin, to put things right rather than to stop the behaviour with 'no'

M in a Group Session

- lot of noise changing activity
- very easily distracted
- doesn't pay attention, reminders to 'sit and look'
- no attention, no contribution
- attempts to wind people up
- fidgeting, face-pulling, talking to self

Other Points

- very much a one-to-one person
- needs supervision
- likes to use instruments and toys
- ignore outbursts, gain attention
- disappears into 'own world' if not talked to regularly
- likes to take the lead, for example: 'how do he do that?' — very much a trial and error boy — not easy to teach or demonstrate how to do something
- gives up very easily — anything that is difficult or he can't cope with accentuates his problem especially if others aren't managing
- needs to finish task fully before moving on — clothes, teeth etc.
- constantly asks questions — maintaining attention, train of thought
- ignore silly comments on stories
- short, stimulating activity — maybe using an instrument of some sort
- tokens — understands? needs more basic reinforcement, for example: ticks?

This kind of observation may help to decide in what circumstances a child may work best. It may also help to make decisions about how to help the child in situations s/he finds most difficult. For whatever reason, the observations should be read carefully and decisions organized to fit into the major management framework.

In summary what would a general observation do to help you in making decisions about ways of helping the child? Once you recognize some of the difficulties, what behaviours will need training up over time and how can you more easily accommodate the more difficult ones?

A Focused Individual Observation — From the General to the Particular

Isolating behaviours and finding out about when and how they occur is not easy. Initially, you have to find out which behaviour is the one that is important to watch. Time is a factor and being sure why you are wanting data and what you

Figure 3.1: Observer sheet — co-operative play

Observer sheet — co-operative play

Date _____   Group colours _____   Leader target | N/A | A | M |

Leader Target 1 _____

2 _____

Minutes	GROUP _____						GROUP _____						Comments
	1	2	3	4	5	6	7	8	9	10	11	12	
Activity													
(a) Leader target													
(b) Leader positive													
(c) Leader negative													
(d) Leader silent													
(e) Group sharing activity/talk													
(f) Group standing/sitting													
(g) Group on task													
Number of children removed													
Number of tokens given for twelve minutes			[ ]						[ ]				

will do with it is a complete process on its own. There is no doubt that using an observation schedule like the one on page 55, can help you to make a more focused decision about how you want to help a child.

Particular Observation for Individuals and/or Groups

Timed observations are particularly difficult but in a busy day it may be that only a ten minute observation is required. Making group observations means that observers are looking for very different kinds of responses. Figure 3.1 is from Co-operative Play (Burnard and Nesbit, 1995) and accumulates information about a whole group.

All boxes that are to be ticked are dependent on all the children remaining in the group. Figure 3.2 is about getting information about group reactions to various teacher approaches. It is specifically designed for only that purpose.

What Shall I Do About It?

The planned consequences of a behaviour are what we call contingent action that brings about relatively permanent positive developments in the behaviour over any amount of time. It is important to consider what was written earlier, that a record of sequence of events should include both the child and adult behaviours. This is important when planning responses contingent to the behaviours of the child/children and necessary antecedents that will affect these

Figure 3.2:   *Reactions of group to teachers' approaches*

Actively Involved

Activity   Date   Time

Number of children in the group

Observation of adult testing changes in intervention techniques to encourage attention to task in the EBD child.

On Task   OT   Off Task   OFT   Verbal Prompt   VP   Tangible   T

Physical Prompt   PP   Active Involvement   AI   Token   T   Social   S

Minutes	y/n	1	2	3	4	5	6	7	8	9	10
Introduce the task. Does the child/children understand the task?											

Record box each minute, type of intervention and 'on-task' for one child (unknown to teacher)

behaviours. When the regular response changes, then the patterns of the previous behaviour will develop positively within a process. Many teachers say that they do not have time to work out all these plans when they have the curriculum to prepare. However, most say that they are unable to impart the curriculum efficiently to disparate classes in terms of behaviour. This kind of planning is essential to class readiness and teacher success.

Perceptions of Behaviour Management

Sharing different perceptions can always be fruitful. The following list was an amalgamation of ideas from thirty adults working in schools as support teachers. They had come together to think a little more about how they could be more supportive to teachers with children presenting difficult behaviour.

First of all, they were asked how they regarded behaviour management. Whilst they all contributed one statement, each one statement provoked a great deal of discussion. The list of statements follows, perhaps the reader would like to consider what each statement means to her or himself:

Perceptions of Behaviour Management — A Sharing from People Working Together:

- The Antecedent-Behaviour-Consequences style of behaviour management is prominent.
- Praising another child exhibiting the desired behaviour is an effective strategy.
- Internalized independent control is the desired end product, not external controls. This statement focuses on the need for behaviour management as a training approach rather than one of control.
- 'Catch them being good' is an effective strategy; unfortunately a long time period is needed for this and like all areas of management needs to be consciously and consistently carried through.
- Would 'behaviour co-operation' be a better term than behaviour management or a combination of the two?
- Many ways of managing behaviour are effective, as many styles as people. However, the sharing of and ability to define methods into a whole school approach improves the effectiveness.
- Children behave differently in different contexts with different people. It is important that no one person is responsible for any one child's behaviour.
- Consistency of approach with a child is essential. Inconsistency breeds uncertainty.
- It is important to separate the child from the deed and promote positive responses to preserve a child's self-worth.
- A rule should state what a child should do and not what the child should not do.
- Having information about the range of syndromes, behavioural difficulties and related factors (environment, genetics) helps an adult to make decisions about the appropriate kind of behavioural management.
- Over-emphasis on the child's ownership of inappropriate behaviour can cause anxiety in a relationship with a pupil.
- Behaviour is affected by how you feel within the group as well as messages received from the group. Encouragement, peer positiveness and language all play a part in this.
- If a child does not receive rewards or achieve targets then the adult is responsible for seeing that the child is placed in positions to achieve.
- Behaviour is primarily a social interaction influenced by factors within the child and outside the child.

- There is a tension between managing violent behaviour and allowing expression of feelings.
- It is necessary to be interested and committed to behaviour and learning behaviour in particular if you want to manage your classroom.
- Negotiation is necessary to change behaviour but the process must be seen as developmental and evolving.
- A child's behaviour often depends on our response.
- It is important to recognize the position of adult and child in a behaviour situation.
- Eye contact is an important feature of talking, listening and managing behaviour.
- A pupil's behaviour affects others in the class — ignoring is not often seen as a fair option. However, ignoring does not mean turning a blind eye. There are ways of ignoring and controlling the behaviour.
- It is difficult to help an adult to see that strategies do work especially when it means changing adult behaviour.
- Some behaviours evoke strong responses in adults and therefore reinforce the inappropriate behaviour.
- Children may have feelings about unfair treatment; adults must listen.
- It is important to manage all behaviour that is appropriate as well as inappropriate.
- Placing children into situations that isolate them in the eyes of their peers, is damaging to the child.
- Self-awareness is crucial for teachers, particularly in dealing with problem behaviours.
- Behaviour is the foremost difficulty in the minds of parents with children experiencing multiple difficulties. It is important to consider the parents' self-esteem and give them something they can do.
- Some children do not respond to the usual strategies.
- Solid relationships are essential for pupil progress.
- Respect for the child as an individual is vital but so also is the child's place in the social groupings.

Conclusion

Raising interest in how a teacher observes the class is the start to organization. Thinking about what input is needed to make changes to encourage positive teaching can be the ingredient missing in many classrooms. Teacher skills begin by looking at a child who is speaking to you and carefully observing a behaviour that is disruptive. Our perceptions vary as do our understandings from our perceptions and teachers need to share those perceptions so that they are clear about each other's approaches to young children. Our observations and perceptions are crucial to teaching, to our understanding and to our more consistent responses to classroom behaviours.

4   The Process of Structuring Your Group or Individual Targets

Introduction

I have been talking to teachers about managing classroom behaviour. Most say that they do not have time to think about targeting certain children's behaviour. In the end, they felt it was better to respond to it as it occurred. As an example, with a child who continually calls out, is it easier to give him or her three chances and then exclude the child from the class until he or she is ready to come back? This method sometimes works but invariably the child will find another behaviour as an annoyance. In the best world, it would be terrific to work on children whose behaviour was exemplary, but usually it is noted and ignored as it isn't a problem. Often and unusually, it would seem, it is easier to reward negative behaviour with attention than positive behaviour. Taking time to deal with one child's behaviour and working with a child who needs help with more simple learning tasks must be rewarding because adults choose to take this root as a response in class rather than work with the children who are on task and who are listening. Being involved continually in aspects of control and children presenting difficult behaviours, and talking to experts, some of whom are employed to go into the classroom to help teachers, it comes as a surprise to me that many teachers do not also have a working knowledge of the language of behaviour management. But is it such a surprise? Teacher training has never focused on this aspect of the teacher's role. Often the volume of preparation and the pressures to cover areas of the curriculum can keep a teacher busy with the majority of children and to respond to the minor difficulties as they arise. However, there are many kinds of behavioural problems from ADDs (Attentional Deficiency Disorders) to Tourette's Syndrome, from conduct disorders to language disorders, that affect behaviour that may need more than just the passing daily acknowledgments both for the teacher's and the child's survival in school.

Task analysis is a basic exercise in focusing attention to detail. Used originally to help in the teaching of more basic behaviours which are given here as examples, it can establish an understanding of how targets are part of a process and the developmental approach to training behaviours that is needed.

This chapter is in two parts. The first deals with task analysis and planning interventions in the classroom. The second is about how to relate task analysis to targeting, what targets are and how they work for individuals and groups.

The most important message will be that the setting of the target is important but it is *how* the adult helps the child to achieve it that is paramount. Both these sections act as an introduction to further more intense methods of diagnosis as a route to planning targets and intervention.

Finally, emphasis is given to the notion that although recent years have seen a concentration on individual targeting for children who are having difficulty learning in the classroom, there is a move to concentrate on targets that integrate the child into the social groupings rather than isolating the child's behaviour from the group.

Task Analysis

Task analysis is a fundamental method of breaking down areas of learning into sub-skills in order to learn more about the task and its difficulties as well as to make a more educated decision in isolating the area in which a child may be having most difficulty. It also shows the direction in which the child might need to go to develop a skill, and focuses on the most appropriate target with which to begin. At first, this may seem to be a lengthy method for making decisions about a child, and, time consuming. However, it should be recognized that, like all other skills, the teacher will only do this exercise mentally but the choice becomes more conscious than haphazard. They may also feel that the child then appears to be having his or her behaviour broken down in a robotic type fashion. This is also a myth. The beauty of it is that it insists on focusing on the individual child's or group's needs. Again, a teacher approaching a problem in a way that will help make changes or situations better for children can get more job satisfaction and, in the end, a more confident result. If anything, the excitement of wanting to know how a process works is enough to look forward to the next day!

A simple example of task analysis might be;

Target behaviour:	To eat with a spoon from a bowl
Pre-entry skill:	Ability to recognize and to name bowl and spoon To move arm and hands with verbal prompt from adult
Criteria for success:	Child can repeat process within a set period with verbal prompts only

1 place open hand on table
2 move hand toward spoon
3 move hand over spoon
4 put hand on spoon
5 close fist over spoon

6 grip spoon
7 lift spoon to bowl edge
8 move spoon to centre bowl
9 place spoon, tipped into bowl
10 move spoon to fill
11 take spoon to mouth

Considering a task analysis of getting out of bed in the morning, the whole act seemed so complicated that it is amazing we all are to even start the day, let alone complete the complexities of it.

Naturally the behaviour problem could be more complex, the kind of activity that one might find in the classroom. For instance a child may show that he cannot move across the classroom without causing a major problem. A task analysis may look like this;

1 child to receive direction whilst sitting
2 child to show that s/he has heard direction
3 child to stand
4 child to walk toward objects
5 child to walk around tables
6 child to pass other children
7 child to reach the object and remember what to do
8 child to reverse procedure to return to table
9 child to sit in chair
10 child to return to work

Most teachers hearing these steps recognize the difficulties a simple direction can cause within a classroom. Even if the child can achieve steps one to six without causing any difficulties, s/he may have forgotten the reason for crossing the room.

Targeting

Connecting task analysis to targets is a simple matter. Terms that are connected to targeting are target *modification*, target *consolidation*, and target *replacement*. Looking back at the first example, we may choose step 11, encouraging the child to take the spoon to the mouth, as the child's target. If after the time allotted, the child has not reached step 11, then the target is deemed too difficult and needs to be modified. Perhaps the child has only reached stage 5, in which case the modified target would be line 6. If after the time allotted, the child has achieved the target but not consistently, then it can be repeated in order to be consolidated. Once consolidated, the target can be replaced, perhaps by the next step or a completely different behaviour.

It is not always necessary to write down the set of objectives into a task analysis. In time, it becomes second nature to break down the behaviours to make it easier for a child to achieve and for an adult to understand the process and choose reasonable targets for the child to achieve. Attempting to give a child the aim as a target is usually doomed to fail. The aim is often too large for the child to reach as quickly as the teacher would like, so the teacher picks up the child's reticence and becomes disillusioned, or else the teacher cannot make the enormous effort it may take to achieve this as well as coping with all the other children in the class. Small achievable steps are best for all.

- If you want to check that a target is worded appropriately, in other words is it a target a child can achieve, put the words 'the child will be able to . . .' in front of your target.

- Remember that you must be able to quantify the target. It should not say for example, 'the child must feel he can succeed', or 'child to say to himself, "I must not be angry"'.

- Remember that the target must be within the child's reach and task analysis will help you to aim the target close to the child's ability.

Targets are part of a whole process that includes;

1 identifying the specific behavioural deficit or excesses
2 determining the baseline rate of the behaviour
3 identifying the situational variables surrounding the child's behaviour
4 devising an intervention strategy modifying these environmental factors
5 monitoring behaviour progress as part of the ongoing evaluation of the intervention, and, if indicated
6 making adjustments in the intervention strategy

Whether you are finding an individual or a group behaviour presenting problems, your approach will be the same. However as we see later in programming, you need to let the child or group be aware of what you are doing and to be consistent. A target should always look to the future development of the child or group, not to immediate success because life is not like that and the adult will have to say, I've tried everything, and nothing works', but to the way in which you can see the child could manage in time. When you enjoy Christmas and eat and drink a lot and gain pounds in ten days, it can take months to work it all off. A child has had a long time of prime learning time and s/he is not going to change overnight.

Targets are not magic but they do give a child a sense of belonging, a sense that people are particularly concerned. A child who helps shape his target, who keeps it on his desk or in his drawer and who can talk about it to parents and teachers, will appreciate the attention it brings. As will be discussed, the target's success, however, lies with the adult.

Aspects of Targeting

Choosing the target is one thing, but that is not where the adult bows out. In fact the most important thing to remember is that a child never achieves just by luck. The target is as much for the adult as for the child. If the child had known how to achieve they might have managed already. It is up to the teacher to teach to the target as you would to any part of the curriculum. How a child is managed and how s/he is helped to achieve is up to the 'plan' or as we call it, the recommended handling by the adult.

The way in which a target can be reached can be as creative as time, the behaviour required and resources allow. There are behaviours for every second of the day for as many people and situations as there are in the world. There are behaviours that appear to be appropriate in a home, in a country and not in another home or another country. Examine the situation in school and classroom, add to that the subjective point of view, and focus on what is acceptable behaviour that promotes learning in that particular environment and what does not. How important it is to the child to change or develop more appropriate behaviours is dependent on the adult's commitment.

Consider this situation. It may be that in PE the children are required to find a space and sit in it. It is important at that time for children to listen to instructions. Problems may occur;

- the space is too big for some of the children to manage their behaviour, to sit still,
- words are lost in a big space,
- it is hard to see all the children's eyes to show they are listening, and
- there are a couple of children who cause problems when far from the normal constraints of a group or teacher proximity.

It is necessary to think about the management of the two children who cannot cope in this situation. It is important to have control of the situation before the lesson starts, so early decisions need to be made about managing the situation and targeting the class or the individuals:

- children could change in the classroom and sit in a small group while being given first directions and ensuring that everyone understands,
- when changing task in the hall, call the children together first,
- make targets for the two children and make sure that they understand that they are part of a plan to make things good for themselves and others, (remember to take a baseline to make sure that these children are presenting a problem) and
- these targets may be part of ongoing problems that the children have and these targets can be seen as part of a process over two or three terms.

Targeting in Practice

Richard

Now to consider more particular problems. One child, Richard, is presenting problems that are exciting a few others. The main difficulty is that Richard is not able to listen with comprehension to directions, and therefore does not know what he is looking forward to doing in the gym. Find the sequence of the re-occurring problem and focus on the step that creates the difficulty.

Target: For Richard to repeat initial directions and comply once in PE

This is a starter, not too big, something Richard can understand. What will you do?

- give Richard a few minutes coming in from play, tell him what your expectations are,
- draw a picture of a clock with the number of minutes you are expecting him to manage at the beginning of the lesson,
- show him that at the end of class if he complies, he gets an extra go on the horse, which he loves.

Break it down, what other ways will help him achieve this target?

- you can manage two minutes off your break to talk to Richard before PE,
- when you explain to the whole group make sure Richard is near you and you are giving him eye contact,
- ask him to repeat the directions and quickly confirm your expectations when he gets in the hall.
- make sure you congratulate him when he complies and do not forget his reward,
- if he doesn't achieve, remind him of the expectation and the reward he has missed.
- *Make sure you help him achieve next time.*

Have you got any plans for the next target that will be contingent on his success?

- is listening and complying to directions an overall problem, are there other times that you can focus on?
- is it just PE? In which case, start a plan that targets him to listen and do more times than once, then for all the time,
- release him slowly, diminishing actual rewards and extending the time you expect him to comply.

Long term aims:

- let him move away from you as he becomes more independent.

Teachers on a course asked if Richard has to listen to the first direction in the gym and then his behaviour falls off-task during the lesson, will he still get the reward at the end of the lesson? There are four possible answers to this question:

1   It should be made clear to Richard that the reward is for specific behaviour — he should be reminded at the end why he is getting the reward.
2   You might praise him for managing the start and say that he must stay with you until the end. You hope to lengthen the compliance with each lesson.
3   Knowing he is getting a reward may keep him on task.
4   You may hold his hand and walk him through what you require of him while directing the other children for the first and then control his co-operation to the end.

Always remember the whole class, and praise them for their contribution toward an enjoyable lesson. Set up situations that are manageable and that will help the child. Remember to think about how, when and where to start targets and plans. Only start if success is certain and remember the techniques of rewarding or ignoring inappropriately or things will become worse.

Child A

Problem: Child A has continual verbal and facial inputs to other children to manipulate them into inappropriate behaviours. Negative self image and negative comments about others. Targets which focus on parts of these problems as starters may be as follows; (The adult recommended handling is after the target)

1   *To talk about helping others*
To give A responsibility to help someone and then later to ask what it was that was helpful. The adult to say to A when s/he needs help, 'Do you need my help?'.

2   *To say nice things about what others are doing*
Adult to model saying good things about other's work. To encourage A to talk about others' work and to help give him/her the words to describe it.

3   *To make smiley faces at people when I say good things*
Adult to do some work on happy and sad faces. Adult to go around the class asking children to make good comments to each other. Adult to comment how good the child looks and give attention when faces are not being made at other children.

Child B

Problem: Can't finish playtime properly and be in the correct place. Needs adult to chase him and bring him back into class. Targets related to the problem.

1   *To be on the wall at the right time to get my token* (could be — to line up and get social reward if tokens are not the system)
Adults to make sure that they have B by the hand two minutes before end of play is called.

2   *To stay on the wall and come in sensibly*
Adult to help B by controlling his going in and praising when he does so. Adult to lessen control but keep giving verbal prompts over a period of five weeks.

3   *To get more stickers on my playtime chart*
Adult to encourage B to put his own stickers on. This target is fundamentally little to do with playground behaviour but to help B enter and settle into the classroom which he finds difficult without a major problem with other children.

Child C

Problem: The child is obsessively sorting out anything near him irrespective of who it belongs to. This means he is off task and annoying others.
Targets related to the problem and how the child will be helped to achieve them.

1   *To keep my sorting for an allotted time*
Adult to have three times a day when sorting is appropriate.

2   *To sort only my own things*
Adult to remind C when he attempts to sort articles that are not his own. Adult to ask C whose objects are they and ask, 'Are they yours?'

3   *To keep my things tidy*
Adult to have a consistent routine that helps C to recognize times in which he must look after his things. Times like: putting shoes away, putting work into own drawer, putting PE clothes into a bag, hanging coat up.

The above example is one that is individual. Many teachers will say that they have ten other children who are also not attending. How can they manage to run a programme for all those children single handed? If this is the case, then the teacher must put a management control programme into action before even considering the other elements of teaching. The ethos should be decided before term and then the schedules, teaching plans, resources and use of adults can build onto a strong framework. Consider targets, they don't need to be a 'by the way' addition to teaching. All the children can have an aim for the month or term. Those who have extreme difficulties are not singled out then, they are part of the policy. All the children can discuss what they feel they need to work on, they can write down their targets, draw pictures and put them on their desks. The whole class can have an aim for the month. The teacher can stress working together, can give the children a sense of purpose, can stress co-operation and sharing, can sit children in pairs if their targets coincide to help each other. Nothing is built in a day, but when a teacher has control of this kind of planning with a difficult class, it will lead to a continual ability to plan a working classroom.

Learning Behaviours in the Group

The concept of knowing where a child needs help and focusing on that area of need by targeting and then targeting plans with ways of helping the child achieve can be a rewarding aspect of teaching. However, it is as important to recognize that the child or children must develop better ways of learning within group and class situations and the best way is to see that a child's target often holds training elements for all children and can be woven into activities that could benefit each child. The teacher who manoeuvres a child with behavioural difficulties into a group activity and can include all children in a class praise is moving in the right direction. Children who are included as insiders will have good feelings, those who are excluded will continue to be so. Placing children into situations in which they can socialize, trains up necessary behaviours for success. The old adage of not removing the household plants when a toddler starts moving around but teaching the toddler how to respect the plant and its place in the environment still holds. Taking away the training resources is never beneficial. Taking away a child's peers with whom s/he is not relating will not help him or her to relate.

For a child, the pleasant consequences of desired behaviour has two roles; they confirm that the behaviour followed was appropriate and s/he would know what to do next time. Group praise is fair to those others who often lose out as well, and should they feel a certain resentment that the louder class member receives the attention, then this strategy can allow them to see that member is following the same rules and receiving attention equally. An overall consistency of this kind can be practised in a variety of situations and in this way, the teacher can help the children with problems to discriminate between cues provided by different settings. The child as part of the group will feel more positive about using his or her peers as models.

Learning Behaviours in Class

In the real world in a class of twenty-five to thirty children, transfer from one stage of ability to learn to another does not follow a unified and clear-cut sequence. Different children may be at different stages of learning and this applies to types of behaviour. Some children may work for natural consequences on entry whilst others may need additional reinforcers and feedback. When children enter school, teachers assume that they have developed learning behaviours. These common learning behaviours develop through usage and less rarely 'consciously' through the teacher's training.

Common learning behaviours include; listening, attending, sharing, co-operating, looking, responding appropriately, sitting in a group, sitting to task, moving around the room without problems, respecting property, putting up a hand for attention or signalling appropriately for attention, following directions, understanding rules of play, preparing for work independently, showing work independently, showing enjoyment of peer company.

More specific problems may show themselves for example; short attention and concentration span, poor memory, inability to sit 'in seat', rocks chair, interrupts children working, pinching, tripping children, screaming, shouting in class, drops and breaks pencils, mixes paints and makes messes, admits boredom and destroys own work, controls discussions by continued talk, monopolizing adults. Many of these specific problems are part of the lack of more common learning behaviours. Although, children with these problems may need specific help, they can also be encouraged to learn some of behaviours from group behaviour learning sessions. A good example is that of Circle Time or Co-operative Play as outlined in this book.

The thought of differentiating behaviour and work is hard for the teacher and as soon as you recognize that there is mixed ability in the classroom as well as a variety of behavioural difficulties, then most teachers find it hard to cope with the magnitude of the problems. However you differentiate work, it means that you cause behavioural difficulties for yourself and the children, therefore:

1 Your preparation must take more time and your recording and marking times must be managed. Because of these schedules, the management of time within the class and therefore the management of what is being accomplished in that time affects behaviour in some way.
2 Children often see that other children have easier work, and take up more time; in other words, it seems to them that *easy work = more attention*. It is therefore not unusual for other children then to request the work that seems to receive the most attention and to resent the work that they have been given: that if you differentiate work then you are also differentiating behaviour. 'I want hard work like him' (excuse to not manage — child knows he can't but lowered self esteem in eyes of peers is high — needs to feel own progress is important) 'I want easy work like him/her'.

3   The minute you differentiate work and behaviour, you are on course for difficulties for yourself and for the children unless you are thinking about the whole picture. The teacher may feel that an overall medium of work is best, not too hard for those who can't and not too easy that the clever ones don't learn. Perhaps the teacher feels that this helps the complex situation but does it help all the children in the long run?

A Consistent, Planned Approach to Behaviour Management

Badly behaved classes are more likely to occur where teachers lack clarity about their own everyday rules, and when teachers respond in an arbitrary and random nature to pupil misbehaviour. This most often happens when the control is to task rather than to management.

Difficulties for Children

Unless what is happening in the classroom is clear to the children, they will have problems in defining what is required of them.

Children recognize that the same names are called by the teacher and they respond to that in different ways. Those children whose names are called often make a supportive non-attentive group. They learn ways of promoting the strengths of the group, disruptive ways. If they are also children whose learning is slow, then it doubles teacher time. Simultaneously, the children whose names are not called get support from their peer group which is often distracting and which lowers their listening and practical work. Children on charts have no respect for them, and are often unsure of the connection between the chart and their behaviour, while children not on a chart often don't give peer support, worry why they have no chart and avoid the children who are on a chart. At times they help but often it is to get the attention vicariously. (The children here described are those who are having difficulties themselves. I have observed more able children helping children who have charts to manage, although inconsistently.)

If a child is allowed some behaviours whilst others are not, a poor programme will show a teacher ignoring but not demonstrating to the child the rewarding process for those who stay consistently within the boundaries. When programmes are started for children, and particular children get charts put on the wall the difficulties are, at worst:

- teacher often forgets the chart and is haphazard in recording or does so when the child is not there and thinks of catching up with the child later,
- child is not clear how the stars/faces are earned,
- when the chart is filled, there is nowhere to go.

If work and behaviour are differentiated for the child then it must be:

- part of a total programme over a year, otherwise progress will not be consistent enough to develop strengths in the child,
- not be an isolating situation for the child which makes it harder for the child to see the peer group to be joined, and more difficult to pick up the fundamental rules of social interchange.

Sharing and Communicating

Things only work if you share, with colleagues and with the children. The statements following are like a checklist of what to know when organizing the whole class.

- Not 'does the child know what I expect?' but 'do all the children know what I expect?'
- Do I spend a long time criticizing children who are not managing rather than giving positive acknowledgment of children when they are behaving appropriately?
- I have clearly stated to children what the rules are (three rules at most) and I am always praising the children for keeping to them as a group.
- My colleagues know my rules.
- Do the children see that I am conscious of my own behaviour?
- I need to target what I feel I can help the child/ren with.
- I need to explain clearly to the child/ren and then work on their achievements more than looking for sanctions when they are not managing.
- Try not to take away — taking away comes to an end and becomes more punitive but giving can always safely get bigger.

Planning and Managing Effectively

More effective teachers are more rewarding of positive achievements and draw attention of the class to those achievements. Effective teachers have a few clear rules that are fairly and consistently employed. These rules should have nothing to do with individual behaviours. They should be rules that help children to understand rules. 'All children must keep their feet on the ground.' In this way it is positive. Rules are for all children so that no one child feels isolated.

The class must have a direction in which all children are headed. Instead of isolating children, the scheme is like the National Curriculum, the children have a way of working through the year. This way the goals are the same for all the children, means of achieving them are the same for all the children, but there will be some goals the adult and the children will have to help along the way. In this way, no-one is special, everyone is special.

Individual Targets Are as Important as Whole Class Targets

Targeting the whole class is important, as is making the target achievable.

For example: We will help each other to listen at story time. Ways to achieve this might be:

- that children have partners to sit with at story time,
- all children discuss the story to start with, and
- all children practise listening to shorter stories at first.

Expectations at the end of story time:

- children share the experience, the story,
- they talk with each other,
- they take turns and all receive social praise from the adult.

Another target might be: all children will be able to share and borrow resources and equipment:

- children should show that they can ask and thank appropriately,
- they should be able to share a piece of equipment and make sure it is returned,
- they should help each other with the use of the equipment.

A third target: all children will be able to listen to each other in group work and talk about the topic in hand:

- they should listen and respond appropriately to the adult,
- they should be clear about the language they need to use in order to raise confidence,
- they should be able to answer each other's questions.

The children therefore can be moulded into common causes that are behaviour based. When teachers give attention to children about these particular behaviours, it means that all children are involved in these acquisitions and not just one child. It is commonplace to find that children presenting problems are often further isolated by the help they may be given.

Having adults in to help is often isolating for a child. Adults see it as helpful because it aids the smooth functioning of the classroom, but for the children it is a sign of fragmentation in the classroom and a choosing of 'one' child. If a child is going to have some behaviour differentiation then we are into targets and it is vital to stress that targets are for adults, too.

Attitudes

Often people feel that they cannot accept behaviourally mechanistic ways of working, but the behaviourist mode has moved on since the early days and people have a creativity with programmes that far outclasses the old 'see it reward it'. The creativity of behaviour management is putting children into positions in which they will succeed. That is an important message and it is the manipulation of what you have; time, resources, human resources, curriculum, activities, that builds your management in the school or classroom.

Box 5: Rewarding good behaviour

A child always runs away at the end of play. His target to be in line. Don't leave it to chance. Go out and finish play in a good way with other members of the class, get the adult on duty to be near enough to hand the child to you for that last few minutes. Grab two hands, a ready hand and a reluctant one, take both children to the line talking about the next good thing. Socially reward the child as if he got there on his own. Make sure that there are good things for everyone in the classroom for lining up and include this child. Don't reward the one child. Reward him or her so that s/he is part of the good thing a group has achieved. Try not to isolate a child who has difficulties, work on socialization when possible. If you think that you can't be bothered, or the tea break is more important, or you had to have a quick word with an adult, or you know you can't be consistent, or you don't think it's important for the child to be there anyway, or the rest of the class are managing so what does it matter? If any of these apply then never start because it will confuse the children if it is inconsistent programming. Your attitude will affect the management of your class.

When we are teaching new ways of behaving, particularly educational skills, we do not usually expect children to discover and use the new skills entirely alone, because if we do then we may have to wait a long time. Teachers who plan and who recognize the problems of managing whole classes with complex and varied learning abilities and behaviour, set up materials, explanations and help in such a way that from the outset, pupils have every chance of displaying the behaviours that they wish them to learn. That is, when planning our teaching of new educational skills our first concern is the management of setting events for the children's behaviour. The idea of setting up situations so as to help pupils respond with appropriate behaviour from the outset is perhaps less familiar when dealing with behaviours which are not strictly educational (see your list of common learning behaviours).

Common learning behaviours are those that all children need as they enter school and which develop through usage and less rarely 'consciously' through the teacher's training.

- listening
- attending
- sharing
- co-operating
- looking
- respond appropriately
- sit in a group
- sit to task
- move around the room without problems
- to respect property
- to put up hands
- to follow directions
- to understand rules of play
- to prepare for work independently
- to show work independently
- to show enjoyment of peer company

Teachers may see the following presenting behaviours that make learning difficult for certain children. It is easier for adults to work on the specific learning behaviour that relates to the presenting behaviour. It is possible that quite a number of children may need practice in attending and so the specific child can learn within a group need and may not feel singled out. Working on behaviours like this is just as important as teaching the curriculum subjects. The two need to go together.

- short attention and concentration span
- poor memory
- inability to sit in seat, rocks chairs back
- interrupts group work
- pinching, tripping other children
- screaming, shouting in class
- drops and breaks pencils
- mixes paints and makes messes
- admits boredom, destroys own work
- controlling discussions by continued talk — monopolizing adult

To recap, on some occasions, starting with the target for individual children may be necessary and certainly it is more usual to use his or her behaviour as a starting point. We then look to our own responses and behaviours to help the child develop better ways of coping with the learning situation. It is also useful to help the individual child to develop within the general class expectations so that you train up not only the individual but the individual in a social gathering and those in the social gathering who need to consolidate what they may know already.

Box 6: Towards diagnosing the problems

Which behaviour is the most important one to manage with the child? Sometimes you see a few children exhibiting the same behaviour. Does one work with all the children in the same way? Earlier on it was pointed out that behaviour management has been criticized in that it does not take into account the background of the child and only considers the presenting behaviour. In fact, the management of programmes for children must take many factors into account because individual behaviours may look the same but on close examination will need very different remediation programmes. This is an important area in targeting and it is one that is discussed in the next chapter.

Conclusion

It is important to see behaviour in terms of a continuum rather than as an isolated description. Once a plan for developing behaviour has been decided upon, it is very important that the adult recognizes his or her individual input. That input should be arranged so that it can be practically executed and reviewed within reasonable time periods. When planning your class/school behavioural needs, you need to have:

- a clarity about what is needed
- a balance between the child and the groups
- a target system for your own behaviour and responses
- joint learning behaviour sessions for listening, sharing, talking, on task through games, activities and work so that equal attention is given to all performers.

5   Diagnosis and Remediation Strategies

Introduction

Some people have had poor experiences with their child who has been diagnosed as having particular syndromes, disorders or as belonging to some
category. Diagnosis of behaviour can be definite or very subtle and meeting
a child's needs or remediating the problem can be anything from good teaching
practice to ways of holding a very aggressive child to particular teaching techniques and skills. It is frustrating for the parent to find for instance, that the
child has a severe 'word finding' difficulty which affects the child's socialization,
or to find that he is considered a naughty boy and receives a smiley face if he
manages play without getting into any difficulties. Some adults don't understand that they too need to show him how to learn and to make the connection
between what he has learnt and the smiley face chart. The parent may also feel
the isolation at the gates, the endless list of misdemeanours in school and the
rising negative feelings about the child.

Diagnosis can be easy. In fact more frequently, children seem to be given
titles that are far from the labels that might be given after a long-term observation. Some children who are very slow learners or who have strange or bizarre
responses are quickly labelled autistic or attention deficit syndrome children
when the total picture presents a very different answer. Parents are then dis-
appointed to find that specific special schools turn their children down for placement. Another difficulty is that the child is placed amongst an inappropriate
peer group and given inappropriate treatment.

Finding people who know 'how' to handle the difficulties is another problem altogether. If the right place is found, it is generally decided that the child
can be managed in the main stream sector after all. Often an untrained person is
placed as a one-to-one into the school to help, thus isolating the child further
from his/her need to learn how to socialize. This is not always the case, but
it does happen.

Diagnosis

The number of difficulties that children may have are as varied as each person's
fingerprints. Irrespective of a 'name' one gives to a child's problem, the remediation techniques need to suit the individual and situation. Diagnosis is more

than just a way to classify, it should also be about the process of determining which methods are best suited for a given youngster's problems and at what speed learning can be expected to go and how much consolidation of learning should take place.

Over a hundred reasons can be found to describe children's behaviour that bring them to the attention of their school as children with learning difficulties. However major characteristics are; hyperactivity, perceptual-motor impairments, emotional lability (depression, anxiety), general orientation defects, disorders of attention (short span, distractibility), impulsivity, disorders of memory or thinking, specific learning disabilities in reading, number, writing and spelling, disorders of speech and hearing, equivocal neurological signs. All of the above are distinguishable by certain overt behaviours. Children may not sit still, will fidget, will not attend to tasks, will be withdrawn, keep dropping pencils, continually call out, put up a hand and forget what s/he wants to say, exhibit poor pencil control, inability to colour between lines, hiding under tables, climbing on furniture and I'm sure all those one hundred and one descriptions that could be equated to one or some of the above.

More particular problems like diagnosed brain damage, autism, epilepsy, dispraxia, language disorders, Retts syndrome, Downs Syndrome, mutism, tuberose sclerosis present their own particular behavioural problems which may or may not be handled within a mainstream setting depending on the severity of the difficulty. Further definition of these problems can be found if it is necessary. 'Contact a Family' publish an excellent catalogue that presents various syndromes and difficulties clearly. These difficulties are more likely to be found within the special school although there is a trend to integrate children who can manage the very demanding timetables of the main stream school. Sometimes it may just be the language and the speed that directions are given, or the confusion of a lot of children, that can make integration difficult for some children.

As a teacher you may come across the following categories; aspergers, Tourette's, ADD/HD, dyslexia, conduct disorders, oppositional disorders or perhaps mild cases of cerebral dysfunction that are often seen as presenting behaviour difficulties. More frequent behaviours would be the transient problems which children may present, that you may see and comment on one day and realize several months later that there is no longer a problem. All children within the realm of development will show behaviours that are not 'what you might expect' from that child. A child who has been on task in the classroom, may find that looking for friends is important and bring that need into the lesson. Once friendship becomes assured, the child will go back on task. A child may worry about a problem at home and become dreamy or off task then, when the anxiety passes, the child may resume previous behaviour. This would be a case of careful observation. Is it a behaviour that could lead to further problems, do you know of any social reasons why the child is exhibiting these behaviours? Should you do anything about it, or is it a 'phase?'

Some specific disorders are characterized next, but this is nothing like a complete list.

ADD/HD (Attentional Deficit Disorder)

If you look at the literature on ADDs you will find that the descriptions might fit many children you have known or know. This is not unusual. Some of the behaviours are those you might see in a child presenting transient behaviours. However, like all aspects of life, it is the degree to which the behaviour presents itself that is important. A person with ADD presents him/herself as having an inability to pay attention, control impulses and in many cases to regulate motor activity. It is most often associated with under-achievement and severe behavioural difficulties. The person may be very aggressive and over talkative. They might also appear to be unaware of what is going on in class. S/he is often unreliable and forgetful. ADD has been popularized in the USA and is steadily gaining attention in this country as, some say, an alternative description of children with emotional and behavioural difficulties. However, its description is far more focused and in many ways does not include the environmental features that may be important factors in children with emotional and behavioural difficulties. It also wipes out the more subtle diagnosis that may also present certain features of ADDS but need a very different approach. It stresses management controls and therefore misses on the idea of managing other therapies or approaches. This attitude also does not alert the adult to the many other reasons for the child's difficult behaviour.

It is easy to fit the child into the category but is it the right category for the child? It is also easy to give parents the false impression that the label ADDS makes the problems better. In fact it means far more input from parents than they might be prepared to give. If you look at what you can do to help, you will see that a lot of the remediation is to do with good teaching. If you are conscious, however, of what and how you are helping, then your teaching also will automatically improve. Your behaviour, your preparation and your understanding and observations will improve classroom behaviour.

There are ways in which to manage the children presenting these problems, some of which are the following; think about where you sit the young person, in a quiet area or near a child who can help. Give the child shorter tasks, with praise for completion, make a contract between adult and child about how much work can be expected and accomplished. Make sure instructions are clear and the child can tell you what they are. Ignore small misdemeanours and increase rewards and consequences. If a child is finding his or her control difficult, give them a place to go to regain control. A child also may find it difficult to change from one task to another or from one area to another, s/he may need closer supervision. If you see frustration building, move in quickly to relieve the overload. There are many other ways in which you can help such a child and you may find information under the following names, Ideus and Cooper (1995) and Cooper and Ideus (n.d.).

Box 7: Need for care in diagnosis

A group of children went to Duxford Air Museum. One child in particular was described by the teacher as hopeless, swift, and couldn't look at anything for any period of time. The child might be a candidate for the label ADDS but on closer inspection the picture is very different. ADDS is what he may be presenting but the difficulties are much more complex. The child's life has been totally fragmented; difficult mother, a series of foster parents, a series of schools and at nine years of age, even with the most consistent and structured reading programmes, has a difficult time recognizing his first phonics and initial blends. His vocabulary is very restricted and his early play techniques are still solo, with an adult. The child's understanding of his world is confused, with his limited language he has no way of translating all the stimuli. The shapes and wonder of large machinery have no relevance to his life.

Asperger's Disorder

This disorder is characterized by having difficulty with reciprocal social interaction and abnormal patterns of communication. However, if these are highly significant then the child is not likely to have Asperger's. Behaviour and interests are often restricted, stereotypic and repetitive. Unlike autism however, there is no general delay in language or cognitive development. You may find that the child is unusually clumsy. It is important to accept the difficult behaviours that the child may present and to 'teach around' the problem.

Dyslexia

This is characterized by poor reading skills that are not necessarily attributable to inadequate schooling, poor vision or mental age. Spelling and reading are affected and sometimes the difficulty is aligned to early speech and language disorders. There may also be other problems such as poor school attendance and social adjustment. The teacher may be conscious of a child's difficulty in rhyming or recognizing letters of the alphabet or the sounds of the letters. Much has been written about dyslexia and difficulties can be seen in the more mature child's writing in reversed letters and words, wrong words read and slow reading rate. Good teaching skills, consistent and repetitive teaching is often the best approach. Do not confuse a child who is a slow reader or whose behaviour has affected their early English skills with dyslexia.

Conduct and Related Oppositional Disorders

Conduct Disorders

This category is about dissocial, aggressive and defiant behaviours. The behaviours include excessive levels of fighting or bullying, cruelty to animals or other people, destruction to property, fire setting, stealing, repeated lying, truanting, frequent and severe tantrums, defiant provocative behaviour, severe disobedience. These behaviours should be observed for six months or longer. It is very hard to manage such children within a classroom at the more severe end of the spectrum. In a sense, it means that very early and rudimentary rules have to be worked on as a basis for building on. A programme for such a child should be school wide with adult co-operation and singular in approach. Building up good behaviours would have to be a well thought out process.

Oppositional Disorders

Usually seen in children below nine years of age, this disorder is characterized by defiant, provocative or disobedient behaviour. The child is usually negative, angry, resentful and hostile. He or she defies adult requests or rules deliberately to annoy other people. The best way to plan progress for these children is to prepare them for activities or expectations to come. It is best to reduce levels of strong directives in order to help the child to get used to a very calm atmosphere where he cannot practise those more hostile behaviours. All positive responses should be given frequent but no boisterous social rewards. It is only possible to be general in advice but it presents a strategy that you may like to consider when you are planning a programme for such a child.

Presenting Behaviours May Need Individual Strategies

Children exhibiting certain behaviours should not be immediately considered for the same strategies or targets. It is possible to make mistakes that promotes failure if you do not consider the child behind the presenting behaviour. Here are some children who are exhibiting the same kinds of behaviours (Figure 5.1). If we explore around the situation more thoroughly, it is interesting to show how targets can vary. Remember that once you have found the targets, you should break down the target and find out ways of helping the child to achieve. Examine XYZTC and observe the pictures as they unfold. The targets that you set for each child will vary. Working on problem behaviours is about finding ways to help the child not to need those behaviours. In Figure 5.1 the behaviours are the presenting statement and the targets are aimed at solving the particular problems. Reading through the process is like reading five different stories. Arriving at the targets has not been a snap decision. A blanket response for all the children would not have arrived at results for the children in the long term.

Figure 5.1: Similar presenting behaviours and resulting outcomes

Name X Age 10 1. Observed behaviour: Kicking, bullying, destructiveness controlled/provoked/unprovoked	4. Other methods, therapies, tuition a. Token Economy System (TES) Inconsistent in response. Would like to achieve without working for it. b. Family guidance/social worker/Family Service Unit input c. Extra gym lessons — offered locally/sports centre d. Police — can they offer something positive? e. Any local activity centres that might offer support? Anywhere he can have responsibility? f. Learn a positive language control	5. Possible behaviour management strategies with choices a,c,f. i. Begin special gym classes ii. Gym classes to be earned with tokens iii. End each day with talk with adult about good things during the day iv. Talk about good things after each session v. Find a motivating activity in the evening that would motivate X vi. Ask X to help someone during the day and talk about it vii. Have a special relationship with one or two adults	6. Child target To be able to share positive activities and friendships 7. Adult-recommended handling To be firm and praise about the completion of tasks To remain calm when talking with X To place X in a situation in which he can enjoy himself, and talk about it later.
2. Frequency/baseline 6 x day	choice a,c,d,f.	choice i, iv, vii	Review period 5 weeks
3. Factors relevant to 1 Out of control at home Police record Older brother in EBD residential school Younger sister, poor physical development Mother at home 'Dad' lives locally On streets at weekends	Reason To help improve self image To form a positive link with the community	To train up areas that can be developed and improve ability to verbalize problems	Recording frequency record all kicking daily

Figure 5.1: *(cont'd)*

Name Y Age 11	4. Other methods, therapies, tuition	5. Possible behaviour management strategies	6. Child target
1. Observed behaviour: kicking, bullying, destructiveness controlled/provoked/unprovoked	a. TES Enjoys collecting but denies interest in spending on activities. Is acquisitive however and enjoys 1–1 in the evening b. Family guidance c. Small group work d. Art therapy e. Boys' Club/scouts	i. To take on two responsibilities around the school ii. To be encouraged not to thumb suck during agreed periods in school time iii. To participate in a group and to answer one question (closed initially) iv. To encourage positive social overtures around school. Adults to model first v. To be able to talk about growing up when co-operating with an adult positively vi. To be given 1–1 when possible to play games initially with adult, later with one child vii. To work on more representational drawing	To join in a conversation by answering a question and making eye contact. To stop thumb sucking during three classroom tasks of ten-minute periods 7. Adult-recommended handling To talk positively at all times and make eye contact Encourage Y to join in activities. Adult to move toward Y when he starts aggression, rather than to move away.
2. frequency/baseline 3 x day once started can be all day	choice a,b,c,d.	choices i, ii, iii, iv, v, vii	Review period 6 weeks
3. Factors relevant to 1. Home reports no problems. Some problems leaked out but not thought significant. Some indications of overmothering, strong influence. Family very close, one brother. School environment, Y very angry, aggressive and threatening. Can be very babyish and immature mannerisms. All toys are boxed and unopened, stored in his bedroom closet	Reason Needs to be independent and to develop more mature behaviours	Reason To develop areas that are underdeveloped perhaps by choice	Recording frequency Record answers and information from ten-minute morning meeting Record thumbs out agreement, reward socially and give hands more activities

Figure 5.1: (cont'd)

Name Z Age 8	4. Other methods, therapies, tuition	5. Possible behavioural strategies From 4-a	6. Child target
1. Observed behaviours: kicking, bullying, destructiveness controlled/unprovoked	a. TES Very interested. Enjoys earning and saving. b. Age appropriate work to be offered. c. Small group work, withdrawal of all 1–1. d. Medical checkups.	i. To request help appropriately ii. Reward self control and independent task completion iii. To pay token for broken equipment iv. To receive a reward for sitting and contributing in a group (token) v. To work within token system at home.	To ask for help when needed To participate in a twenty-minute group meeting, allowing others to talk 7. Adult-recommended handling To make sure that Z makes eye contact when speaking and when Z receives a token. To say . . . 'S. is talking first, listen' to Z. Praise all independent work.
2. frequency/baseline 6 x day	Choice a,b,c.	Choice i, v	Review period 5 weeks
3. Factors relevant to 1. Similar behaviour home and school Z. had petit mal, would often hurt himself. Parents very anxious and over protective. Gave a lot of attention. At five medical problem became a behavioural problem. Exacerbated by 1–1 attention at start of school. Could not share with other children.	Reason Earning through being on task independently to develop work and behaviour skills in parallel.	Reason Reinforce structure for Z to work within.	Recording frequency Record on two days per week all negative behaviours. Record on-task for two tasks set a week.

Figure 5.1: (cont'd)

Name T Age 9 1. Observed behaviour: kicking, bullying, destructiveness	4. Other methods, therapies, tuition a. Initial inconsistent reaction. Wants to earn but is thwarted by uncontrolled behaviours. Resorts to other ways of acquiring. b. Drug therapies/medication? c. Contact a family — suggest support for parents d. Psychotherapy — has good control of language — may be an outlet e. Art therapy, great creativity but is getting less able to control hands. f. Any other placement for suitable for Tourettes?	5. Possible behavioural strategies i. socially reward and if possible use token when ever co-operative to increase confidence ii. Ignore any residual kicking and destruction (small) at the end of a problem iii. Give particular jobs (social out of class) when completing tasks set iv. Talk about difficulties as they start to arise v. Train up desire for certain activities to increase motivation	6. Child target To be able to talk about difficulties as they start to arise. To earn tokens legitimately 7. Adult-recommended handling To help T into positive situations in which he can earn To keep calm and observant when dealing with T. Always give firm boundaries.
2. frequency/baseline 6 x (30 min duration) day	Choice a,b,c,f.	Choice ii, vi, vii	Review period 3 weeks
3. Factors relevant to 1. Similar behaviour at home. Adopted. Two sisters, one in residential placement. Parents are caring, loving and concerned. Unhappy about sudden turn of events.	Reason T needs to be calm as often as possible and encouraged to concentrate on work rather than on uncontrolled behaviours.	Reason Train up all possible self control	Recording frequency Record all aggressive behaviours, type of aggressive behaviour.

Figure 5.1: (cont'd)

Name C Age 11 1. Observed behaviours: kicking, bullying, destructiveness uncontrolled/unprovoked/provoked	4. Other methods, therapies, tuition a. TES Understands he uses his tokens to get activities but doesn't understand a lot or a little b. SLD placement? c. Gets hot flushes, check epilepsy d. Social skills training/social word training	5. Possible behavioural strategies choice from 4-a,b. i. Make sure all tasks are understood and consolidated before going onto next task ii. C to take part in all group activities making sure he understands directions and turn taking in talk iii. C's tasks to be short and contingent iv. C to have own social skills programme	6. Child target C. to put up hand when he wants help C. to listen and repeat instructions 7. Adult-recommended handling To make sure C has help before he gets too exciteable. To simplify all directions for C. To ask other children to talk clearly when talking to C.
2. frequency/baseline 2 x day	Choice a,b,d	Choice i, ii, iii, iv	Review period 4 weeks
3. Factors relevant to 1. Absent mother from 2 years of age. Functioning between 3–4 years of age. Works himself into excitable highs at school and home. Misunderstands more complex sentences and directions. Lives with Dad, help from Nan.	Reason C likes to belong to a structure that clues him into what is happening next.	Reason C to be as independent as possible for short periods.	Recording frequency A tick sheet for C as he finishes off his set tasks. C to receive tangible reward for a lot of ticks. C to keep a portfolio of work so that he can see it grow.

Remediation

There are many resources and ideas that can be used to train up good behaviours or attention in small groups of children. For most children with difficult behaviours, reading and other academic areas become lost in the move up through the school. Children are given work they cannot manage, or do mindless work that they cannot understand and their social behaviour worsens. Once they are on the move, the difficult part is to stop that progression and start to take hold of the problem where the child is. Small groups must be formed within a school in which attention and phonics are attended to. *SRA, Toe by Toe, Attack,* and other repetitive teaching resources make a real difference to the children when they can succeed and know what and how to learn. Teaching whole classes of children sharing skills based on topic work has been documented by Burnard and Yaxley (1996). Training skills is about being creative and setting up situations in which good teaching and learning can take place.

Strategies Doomed to Fail

Quite often, mistakes are made. The idea of behaviour management often seems easy to people and they take the principles, misunderstand the methods and end up either failing or giving up or the usual cry, 'I've tried it and it doesn't work'. Three systems are explained, all briefly tried and deserted.

Inconsistent strategies with confused criteria   Example one: One method was to give children raffle tickets every time they were 'good'. This was to encourage those with difficulties to keep up with their peer group. At the end of the week, the draw was made and a prize given. In practice, those who were already good earned a lot of raffle tickets. Those who had difficulties with their behaviour, but tried with less success had least chance of winning although they may have had to work harder on controlling their behaviour. These children quickly became discouraged by lack of success. Teachers were not sure what criteria for 'good' was and therefore their giving was varied.

Example two: Lack of criteria   The method was similar although the raffle ticket was just a lucky ticket. The idea was that when a 'good' behaviour was spotted anywhere, the teenagers received a lucky ticket. Unfortunately, again there was no criteria. The children were noticing that they were watched and then did what they felt was a good behaviour and demanded their ticket. Again, some adults gave freely so that they could keep peace whilst others required a much longer example of good behaviour. Children chose to be with adults who gave more freely. There were no rules for if tickets were lost, or if tickets were taken or stolen. When the 'prize' was won, no-one really knew what behaviours had caused that child to win. There was also no record of the tickets gained, therefore no recognition for children who may have worked very hard through the week.

Need for specific rewards: Another example is that of adults giving a child points from one to ten from the whole the week from reflection on the Friday. If there are no specific criteria, then this system will be unreliable in rewarding behaviour and will not present a true record of behaviour. It is not possible to be accurate considering inconsistencies in both your memory and children's behaviour.

A successful system evolves over time, it has rules and boundaries, it is known by all staff and children, it is reflected on and modified, it can be enhanced or renewed but most importantly, the criteria for reward should be carefully considered and each child should be able to recognize the fairness of the system. Decisions to amend or add to systems should be organized. If any part of a system is mishandled it can lead to escalation from an individual to those watching and taking part following suit. This not only makes it inconsistent it also will lead to its downfall. Each orchestrated section of a structure should be discussed and considered by all those involved. Structure is about sharing, from the building, to the practical running and management of the rules and boundaries to the development of staff and children. From large to small, everything is significant.

Conclusion

Presenting behaviour often hides the true nature of the disturbance. Before making decisions about the overt behaviours it is best to examine all the issues before you decide on targets that children can achieve. Managing your class-room is about being able to co-ordinate a variety of needs, behavioural and academic. It is important that the school is supportive of all decisions made and that adults share plans and programmes.

6 Changing or Developing Behaviour: Be Actively Involved in Managing the Process

Introduction

We always talk about changing or developing good behaviours in children but one of the most difficult things for teachers to talk about is their own behaviour and how they can change that to accommodate the needs of the child/ren. For a teacher to be actively involved means that he or she not only commands a class from the outside but is also involved in its processes. Here we examine the positive aspects of teachers looking at their own behaviour and why that is as important as observing children's behaviours. This chapter also looks at the important aspect of attention, how teachers and children get attention and give attention.

Problem Behaviour

Remember the example of the children lining up in Chapter two? Unfortunately, there are times when an adult may carry on his/her choice which suits his or her behaviour, which is exactly the behaviour that is encouraging the inappropriate responses. This can be done consciously or unconsciously, almost because he or she feels safe with the decision and responses. A behaviour is thus repeated, although it continues to cause a problem for her/him and the children. It may be that the effort required to work on another solution is too much bother, or, that the teacher feels that the particular response is the one that the managers of the school will see and hear as being used appropriately, so that the problem is perhaps seen to belong to one child, not the adult who is determined to win loudly and with persistence. Here it can be seen that adult behaviour may be inextricably linked with aspects of the school other than those directly relating to the children. It is the recognition of a situation as problematic that is significant. When a teacher finds himself or herself repeatedly doing the same thing in response to a problem behaviour without satisfactory results, that pattern may be perceived as unstable and may generate a reason to change.

Talk to any teacher about problems in the classroom and he/she will talk about the child, the resources, the time, the size, the national curriculum problems, number of children but never his or her own problems within the structure. Why? The teacher before all others seems to have to have a sense of infallibility. To share a problem is seen to admit a weakness and yet for most people in the world a shared problem is halved. Looking for solutions to difficulties is to do with communication, and children need to see teachers comparing notes and deciding what to do.

Prevention is a positive plan but it has to be long term and most often, from the very start, adults respond to the behaviours, they do not intervene early enough in the right way. The right way would be to look at behaviours that a young child is lacking and give that child those skills to deal with the learning and social situations s/he meets. Below is an example of how problems grow. We all know they grow like this but we need to consider it carefully in light of our educational system and processes.

The Normal Development of a Problem or What Is the Ultimate Sanction Anyway?

There is always a beginning and before that more beginnings. However, I am going to start at nursery school, but the beginning could also be at birth and before that the birth of the parents and their lives. The development of the problem is limited here to the educational context only. You will see that this leaves a great deal unsaid. Behaviour with all its vagaries can be a subject forever under consideration. These thoughts are about the process of learning that is aided or not by sanctions. Please note that this sequence is based on problems and negative sanctions only.

In the Nursery

When a child is observed to be hurting others, being uncooperative and unsociable. The following happens;

- child is discussed by adults within hearing and without sanctions
- negative reprimand or directions are given
- immediate response and removal of child from potential problems
- child sits with one adult
- child's hand is held
- child is not allowed certain toys or resources because of danger to other children or may break the resources
- child is not invited to play at other children's homes or parties

- child is put at a single table for food or activities
- adults refuse to help the particular child as it is unrewarding
- other parents avoid child's mother
- child's parent arrives to lists of complaints about behaviour

In the Family

Child seen in negative light because of the complaints. Looks for attention via negative reinforcement. At home there may be the following;

- negative sanctions; negative words
- disappointment from adults
- child is often sent up to room, isolated
- child is not allowed on trips, often stays at home,
- adults unaware of effect of negative and positive reinforcements-no training

In the Reception Class

Child appears to have little self control, cannot take directions, unable to play with others and share equipment. Behaviour known from nursery and other parents. The following happens;

- child sits next to teacher
- there is always an adult to hold child's hand
- child sits with assistant at back of class in group talk sessions
- child is not included in activities that need independence, e.g. group plays
- child receives more frequent use of negative language and attention
- child is not encouraged to play with other children in case of a problem
- child is given busy jobs, lots of colouring in
- child is OK if with individual adults

In Class One

Child observed-marked inability to stay up with normal developmental posts in basic English curriculum. Child shows inattention and annoying behaviour toward other children. Shows inability and opposition in carrying out directions. Often calls out and will sometimes hurt other children Major sanctions and special work which often means exclusion from group work. The following often happens;

- one adult to keep child on task
- child hears negative language and raised voice whatever s/he does
- conversations within hearing of child about what differentiated work the child will have that sets him/her apart from the other children
- child has smiley faced charts that others don't have
- other children are told to 'ignore him/her'
- child is often given time out with a special adult
- child has time out to do special jobs

In Class 2, 3 and 4

Child observed; child's reputation goes before him or her, adults already feel that having the child will be a negative experience. Several other children seek him/her out because they have seen that s/he models the kind of behaviour that receives the attention they think they might like. Because of the effect on the other children, the teacher feels that he/she: 1) needs to spend more time with the child, 2) finds as many ways as possible to keep the child occupied in class or otherwise employed outside the class and 3) is past helping and that there is little s/he can do at this stage.

Major sanctions and part-time assistant for child follow. In addition:

- child is given work around school by the management
- child is given a special table in class away from the other children
- child holds hand of adult at playtime and in group discussion times
- child has busy work, colouring in
- child has half-day only in class
- child has some sort of inconsistent reward system for behaviour!
- child misses no assembly
- child cannot manage social situations — no trips out

It is in this time that inappropriate tasks are given to these children and this causes them to over-react which in the end asks for over-reactions from adults. An adult often mirrors the problems of the child in response. It is here that there is less time spent on rewarding success and more on punishing failure to conform. Sanctions are usually some form of exclusion, a day, a few days, weeks or being in school doing activities that the other children recognize as exclusion: working with one other adult, doing busy jobs for teacher/management around school and being allowed in for short periods of time. The 'place' the child might have had in the system is dwindling to a fine thread.

In Class 6: Exclusion

The child has been contained for too long and special school is considered. If not a special school then it may be that starting secondary school with withdrawal into a tutor unit may be the answer.

In Class 7–9

The child is unhappy and is often in fights around the school, is lively in class and can discuss items but then continues to disrupt when teacher changes activity to quiet work. The following frequently happens;

- in detention
- unit work
- stay in to complete work
- sent to head of year
- sent to head
- does jobs around the school
- has special classes
- letter is sent home to parents

Admittedly one of the least popular comments about the sanction policies, is that people use them poorly. One of the reasons for this is poor, inconsistent teaching.

There is a particular 'language of exclusion'. This language is full of emotive words that raise temperatures and promote action and discussion. They are words that help point to the children who grow with negative responses: ignore him, that's best, not good behaviour, stay with your adult, hold his/her hand, don't spit, don't kick, don't shout, this is not good enough, here's your special table, s/he just shouldn't be here, s/he never does as he is told, suspension, expulsion, exclusion, and others can be added.

It is clear that no problem ever 'just' arises at least not a problem that takes on such gargantuan dimensions — the problem of a child who is so difficult that exclusion for three days, or for greater lengths of time, seems to be the only answer. The response reaction is not a preventative action.

The adults in an institution are always there, they do not move up the development ladder and leave, so they have the enviable position of being able to prepare and to put in place ways in which to prepare ground for developing ways of improving situations for managing problems that arrive.

Teachers Changing Their Own Behaviour — How Difficult Can it Be?

Asking teachers to change their own behaviour is difficult. In *Co-operative Play* (Burnard and Nesbitt, 1995) a training ground for social interaction and adult skills, adults are asked at the start to think of a target for themselves. We all find targets for the children with no difficulty, but adult targets are hard. An adult may get out of it by the wording '... *we* are all going to try to learn something about Greek plays today', but it should be strictly '*I* am going to try to make sure all the children know something about ...' or '*We* are all going to share today' strictly should be '*I* am going to encourage the children to share'. In theory it would seem easy for adults to target themselves. For example, 'I speak too loudly, I should keep my voice down', 'I try to hurry my group so there is a lot of frenzied activity whereas my target could be to slow myself down and to pace myself for the twelve minutes'. We all have our faults, or things that we want to do better and for the most part they cause the behaviour response from the children within the system. When adult targeting was first introduced it caused a problem. One teacher went as far as to say that she could find no problem with her teaching. Teaching should be about developing and we can only do this if we admit that there are approaches and skills that we have that can still grow better.

The Need to Feel Safe

I also researched into whether teachers could leave the safe teaching styles that they chose, for other approaches to see if they could get better responses and improved attention from the children.

- So teachers were asked to only say good things in response to children and to ignore poor behaviour. It sounds easy but is, in fact, very hard. Most teachers would be afraid to ignore because they feel that things will escalate out of their control. Ignoring can be many things. It can mean holding a child's hand but not making eye contact or sitting a child at your feet turned away from the other children, still in your control, but not getting any attention.

- Teachers were also asked to do the work with the children and to model active involvement with particular activities. Again, some teachers may not feel safe with this in that it may close the distance between teacher and child and in some way diminish their image, making them seem less awesome to the children and perhaps more vulnerable.

- Teachers were asked to help children in more practical ways, showing them where they were wrong, moving about and giving as many physical prompts as possible. But some teachers like to stay up front, and to rule by less energy and preferring to use the teacher desk as a place children come to.

- Teachers gave Smartie rewards through a lesson, not many, but just enough to make them valuable. Most teachers didn't have a problem with this as it does extend the idea of teacher as giver.

Teachers found it hard to change although it was found that those changes meant more alert children. In fact thinking about changing methods and practically changing them did improve teaching. It was often hard for them to keep up the change in their approaches and controls, although many teachers said that it made them aware of extra strategies that they would feel confident to use as the need arose.

Changing Your Style

Some educational resources suggest learning strategies while teaching. For instance, in SRA reading schemes, the method is to raise a finger and get the children's eyes to follow it to the page. The system is repetitive and depends on a calm, consistent approach with a great deal of success and praise. However, it is not the style that many teachers want. They feel that it is boring, too repetitive for themselves, and also for the children. They feel that the children must be feeling the same way as they do, so they give up the movements that are important for getting the attention. Many adults make this mistake. Children are never bored by what they do well, just as they like to hear well-known stories over and over again. And, from the child's point of view, the system is great; they know it, they are assured of knowing most of it and as already stated, most people learn best when most of what they hear is known to them. Learning a new teaching strategy in one context is useful when generalized to other situations. Changing has to do with learning, practising and generalizing.

Who Benefits from a Change in Behaviour?

Think about it. If you had a choice of 1) changing a child's playtime behaviour by taking him by the hand and starting him off with a game outside with the promise of coming two minutes from the end to give him positive feedback on good play, and 2) rushing to the staffroom to get the cup of coffee and a three minute sit down and back to complaints of the child's poor playtime, which one would you choose? If you decide to give up the time others will not agree with your decision. This kind of behaviour change is hard for adults, even though it is likely to improve the quality of a child's play and encourage a better start to the lesson after play in the long term.

Which Behaviour Are You Rewarding?

When we were talking about adult behaviour in the classroom we saw that it is very easy to reinforce the wrong behaviour, even with conscious effort not to do so, but remember that our actions are always reinforcing one behaviour or another. It takes practice to identify which behaviour you are trying to reinforce and the principles of positive reinforcement should apply here. For example, if a child repeatedly speaks out of turn and his or her teacher repeatedly responds by explaining that the child should wait to be called on, the teacher's response is part of the problem. If every time a child does not hand in his or her homework, he or she is made to stay in at playtime but continues not to hand in homework, the problem is both the student not handing in the homework and the teacher having him/her stay in at playtime. If the responses to a problem behaviour are not changing the problem situation in the long term, then they are helping to maintain it.

Perception and Performance

There are many decisions to be made in the classroom and perception of the problem and interpretation of the problem are the first steps. If the interpretation helps the teacher to change his or her behaviour it will possibly change the behaviour of the child. An individual's perception affects the way s/he behaves. At times it may be possible and helpful to readjust that perception and therefore the response to the behaviour. For example, a non-performing child is seen by the teacher to be lazy and underachieving.

The teacher's response is based on those perceptions. S/he involves the headteacher, the child becomes involved in counselling and psychological assessment and is reprimanded for inattentiveness. Can the teacher understand the child's perception. Would it be useful? A non-performing child may feel that the work is repetitious, boring, not relevant, or too hard.

Another aspect that may cloud a teacher's perception is the tendency to excuse a child's behaviour by his background but this offers no help in changing adult behaviour in the situation. At worst it excuses a non-involvement in offering practical solutions. It is more practical and rewarding to isolate the things that you can change and to adopt a pro-active approach to the management of children.

Differentiating Behaviour

Everyone is now used to the idea that the teacher differentiates tasks in the classroom, but at times differentiation can cause problems. Teachers often spend more time with the child who has learning difficulties, as I heard one person say 'who needs most . . . gets'. Some children look at the easier task and put two and two together. How many times do you hear, 'I can't do this work, can I do what Jimmy is doing?'. Easier work to a child then means more teacher attention. It may not be the more able child who cannot stay on-task, but it may certainly be the less consistent child who is looking for more social help than academic help. If the teacher needs to teach a new task to the children who have progressed further than another group of children s/he knows the work differentiation, but how to manage the class and 'teach on' new tasks rather than setting consolidating work, is a bigger problem. So differentiating work has management implications.

In a similar way differentiating behaviour also pushes the teacher to re-examine the structure of the class. If a teacher makes long-term plans to manage the various factions in the class, then awareness of what is being allowed and what is not may be clear to the teacher, but is rarely clear to the children. A differentiation of behaviour within a class should be a planned process of intervention to maximize potential learning based on individual need. But the process is only as good as the adults' ability to weave the process into the greater learning experiences of the class.

Systems as Part of the Process

Managing your classroom is about devising systems. Changing the structures with new ideas means that the teacher and children must adapt. A system of any kind is about people or resources that work together in a consistent way. Systems provide the structure and environment in which to focus ideas or activities. They also facilitate evaluation. There have to be some rules for systems to work as well as the plans, the objectives and the overall aims. You could say that a filing system in an office is organized and working toward a successful business and in the same way a classroom is organized in order to achieve certain results. A good system should be able to stimulate reflection and development.

A classroom system is only part of a greater system and the two should work in partnership supportively. But both the school and classroom should work to the principles of any good system which means that participants;

- work together/think together
- focus ideas and activities
- create a harmonious environment
- provide a backdrop for evaluation

Behaviour is multivariant and has unlimited description and if some kind of consensus is to be created in a working environment where behaviour is the focal point, then boundaries and structure have to exist.

Systems for Training Social Behaviour

A child may finger feed at home, other children may eat with a fork, or a spoon, in front of the TV at a table, with others outside the family, with the family, in isolation in his room or at the fish and chip shop or restaurant, the combinations and expected level of behaviour will vary subsequently. In a system there can be one or two accepted daily situations to do with eating — around a table with other children and staff or with peers/sandwiches in key worker groups. The system requires the children to behave in a way they

Figure 6.1: *Stumbling blocks to successful targeting*

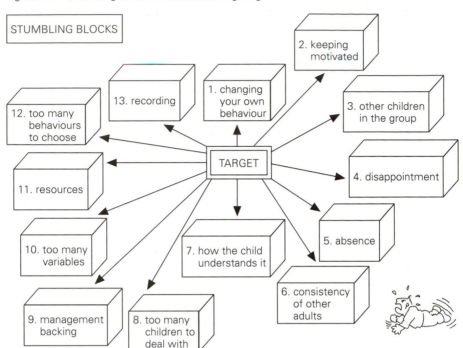

understand over time that will reward them (token) for the method used which requires polite social co-existence. In time, it may be that behaviour will become part of the child's routine. When the child is out of the system the idea that certain behaviours will have been practised may allow the child to use them in his/her own systems (family/outside the family). The child's attitude toward a positive attitude may develop or give the child a course of action that is preferable to the ones he has used previously.

A strong system should allow other areas for its workers to develop as it has formed a unit to work in that then stimulates other things, for example, personality, academic interest, curiosity, personal motivation, opportunities to observe and a place in which to develop. There are always seemingly valid reasons for not joining a system or disagreeing with its aims, which can cause difficulties for others. There can always be opportunities to change or develop that system as long as there is a consensus for change and a mechanism for discussion. Every system has its stumbling blocks, and education is no exception. Within the school, if a decision about a target for a child is taken then the above represent a number of the problems an individual may encounter (Figure 6.1).

A teacher must be very determined to overcome all these blocks, but part of the process is to be convinced that it is worthwhile to do so. This is why it is said that behaviour is not being *changed* so much as *developed*.

There is so much involved in change that the idea is very stressful and can quickly be lost. To develop behaviours shows an understanding of all the processes involved in helping children to learn and develop social behaviours.

System Used in a Special School for Creating a System of Behaviour Management

---

Box 8:   Co-operation in class — the reward

Once a week the children nominate a child in each class to explain a situation in the classroom where all the children have co-operated. All the children listen to each other and ask questions. Then each class gets into a huddle to make one decision about which class they think had co-operated the best. One spokesperson is chosen. Each class votes. If it is a tie, the other classes re-huddle and re-vote. The certificate is awarded for the week.

In the school for emotionally and behaviourally disturbed children to which I am attached, the children are part of an organized system. Most activities are to do with sociability and the training up of language skills to improve behaviour control. As in the example in Box 7 the process of negotiation is linked to behaviour control and the training of social organization. However, because there is a system and whole school understanding, any part of the process is firmly supported by staff and children alike.

If you want to:

- create new systems for your environment,
- adapt teaching methods to suit the system,
- include individual and group programmes in the system.

You will need to:

- research what you want to do,
- organize the system on paper,
- be confident that you know why and how you will do it,
- convince any other people who may be involved that it is the right thing,
- look at timing and resources,
- ask if it can be consistent, and
- reflect on the development.

Adapting Teaching Methods to Suit a System

This may mean making a special time in the day for teaching particular skills, or adapting skills to another system. Time is always a problem for teachers, but the examples given may fit in well with the ordinary curriculum.

- Circle Time — won an educational award for the best social invention. It is based on the fact that the Sioux Indian does everything in a circle. A Circle Time session is one where the children talk, in a circle, about a variety of issues from five minutes to half an hour. It can be incorporated into a whole school policy on discipline and behaviour. You can embellish it with each speaker holding the speaking stone for example.
- You may decide that you will have a helpful fifteen minutes where the children who can do a task help others who cannot. Having made this decision, give it a name, decide how to do it. Decide how to monitor it and start.

Co-operative Play — How Reflection Has Developed this Social System

Most behavioural techniques are not particularly marketable in their present form. They require synthesis into comprehensive programmes or systems designed to attain major educational objectives. So what is marketable is a system of direct instruction that combines a variety of behavioural techniques and specifies how they are to be operationalized. Such a system is the one we have devised which contains behavioural techniques such as positive reinforcement, tangible rewards, cognitive input, social praise, time out and others, entitled Co-operative Play.

What is It?

A system which has adults and children interacting using behaviour management techniques. The main aim is the improvement of social behaviour but it also includes objectives that are educational, based on either the topic or social interactions like friendship or family and so on.

How it Works

1 **Start** — Whole group meeting in which
   - a coloured sticker is given to show to which group you belong. This will not change
   - children discuss what is important about co-operative play
   - the main topic is announced

- four twelve minute activities are described to the children and adults
- adults give their own targets
- groups are dismissed to the activity of their choice. They receive one token when settled.

2   **Activities** — Each activity takes twelve minutes and each group rotates through all.

- time keeper gives a half time and two minute warning and signal to change
- each activity basically drawing, cutting and sticking, a game and model making are designed to be entertaining, stimulating and interesting so that the children want to take part
- token is given at the end of each activity.

3   **Movement** — it is important to line up and move together as a group to the next activity.

- important to finish on time so that the area is ready for the next group
- important to listen well at start so that you know what to do.

4   **Removal and return** — Bouncers' role is involved here, moving around from group to group.

- remove children with minimal disruption
- talk to children about the problem
- remind child of expectations
- return to group and make sure they settle and manage.

5   **End session** — Full groups meeting in which

- a sweet rewards children with group stickers on their sweaters representing the child's ability to stay a member of a group
- observers give positive feedback
- each group invited to show and talk about what they have done and learned.

Both adults and children are expected to show interaction skills (see flow chart below). In this way, children can be aware of all participants taking part as a social and learning activity.

Expectations of behaviour are very simple and are made clear to the children. Adults ask children to think about what they are doing. Whilst the adult consolidates the structure of the sessions by asking certain questions, so those questions can become part of what the child is thinking in order to manage and enjoy the whole sequence of events to the full. Understanding that enjoyment is more fully realised when everyone follows the basic ground rules, is a hard concept for children with behavioural difficulties (see flow chart on page 101).

In the spirit of action research, reflection causes change and developments and the following looks at new additions to the system.

Recent Developments

- adults' target
- addition of facilitators — helpers and display
- older children as helpers — special status/role model
- changing roles to gain experience

Activities
- relevant topics to classroom
- personal aspects
- groups of mixed ability
- motivating enough, special preparation, group v. individual activities
- planned on termly basis

Other
- children's comments
- staff induction includes all roles
- incorporating visitors
- induction of new children, placement, group size, co-operation
- reinforcing work and skills learned in classroom and playground
- adults sharing information — successes, difficulties, planning activities, changes, team work

Co-operative play as a whole school venture, in which the management, care staff and teaching staff are all involved, is an example of the idea of everyone being involved in developing ethos and policies of the school. It is not always possible to establish a situation like this one and its strength lies in the need for staff to work together on the training up of good behaviours in the children.

Co-operative play was developed using reflection as a process. Every new idea, modification or addition was discussed and organized and put into practice.

If the same idea was moved into the main stream setting, you might consider working with another class teacher or with another adult in your classroom. You might want to improve sharing in topic work, the more able with the less able, and you might set up a situation in which this can happen. You might have ideas about a fresh approach to morning assembly that requires a whole staff approach. It may mean changing adult roles or habits in the morning. Think about it. Can you change behaviour to renew a system and help change learning behaviour?

What is Attention all About?

'Standing to attention' reminds one also of the officer in the box, guarding the queen. Body rigid and eyes to the front, never distracted, you can jump up and down, step on his toes, pull silly faces, have your picture taken with him but you will never see the soldier distracted from his attentional duty. How do they manage to stay still and silent? Is it just a case of thinking of other things, of keeping the mind focused on one thing or perhaps a number of things, what training goes into that kind of attention?

'Attention — eyes left' in the army means that the body is rigid with the eyes searching for no other distraction. Once attention is gained, the instruction is given so that the eyes move to the left and then the body is given an order to turn. The order of the execution of events is such that members of the army can act as a corporate body, can follow directions, and when it is necessary can support each other by understanding where each person is which is after all a form of mutual support.

If the intercom says 'Attention . . .' your ears pick up that word and for a time your ears pay special attention to what is being said. If you see the word 'attention' it may be in red and your eyes will automatically read the next piece of information so this word has come to mean something that focuses the senses. It means what you are about to see, hear or do will be important. Of course there are many other complex learning behaviours but the most basic are those to do with looking and listening. The character of a child's learning is indicated by the quality and length of time a child can attend.

Three elements of attention are;

- Gaining a child or children's attention
- Keeping the attention
- Rewarding attention

Three skills that are prerequisites/or need training up to work on attention are;

- listening
- looking
- motivation to learn

These areas are easy to consider but in practice must be organized into the framework of classroom organization and in fact into all school activities by any adult. It is easier to think about these behavioural objectives as part of how you teach. If the approaches are consistent and clear, then the children, with even the poorest abilities, will be able to gain strategies to learn at their own pace.

How Do You Gain Children's Attention?

Teaching anyone is a question of gaining attention. I am very aware as I train adults that it is just as important to get adult attention as it is to get children's attention. I think that the way I get and retain attention is;

- to know exactly what I am going to say
- to be interested in what I will say
- to have the resources ready
- to know the order of the information
- to make the information clear
- to know what each individual will understand
- to know how to make all the class understand
- to reward each and everyone for attending

This is how you might approach a learning situation if all the children have a reasonable level of ability. If you have a class of mixed ability and are considering aspects of attention and motivation the following ideas may help.

Looking

- train up eye contact
- direction of looking
- descriptive language
- length of concentration
- foreground and background
- developing hand eye co-ordination
- train up understanding by asking questions about what is being looked at

Looking at three dimensional objects and working toward two dimensional and flat surfaces could be part of the process, not all children can 'see' a picture. Training looking is linked to training up motivation. To look at toys in terms of what they do, how they are made, what colours they are, who they are for means that an introduction to looking has enjoyment attached to it. Basic information, but it gets more interesting as you expand the idea into other aspects of the curriculum and levels of learning.

Listening

- repetition of sounds
- following directions
- repeating instructions
- being part of a two way conversation
- answering questions
- taking turns talking in a group
- telling part of a shared story
- the ability to sit and listen to a short story
- a longer story
- making lists

Listening relies on other abilities such as looking, sitting, differentiation of sounds, and motivation. Listening is about taking in information, processing it and being able to use that experience to develop learning. Listening should be pleasurable in order to motivate. Tapes and ear phones are a good way to train up listening without distractions so that children can focus on information. Language has a great deal to do with learning, active listening and speaking, the communication of ideas are the basic resources in all classrooms.

Motivation — How Do You Know that Learning Is Taking Place?

The soldier is trained to pay attention to his job. We know he attends to his job because he is not distracted from it. Finding out that learning has taken place gives an indication that a child has attended. Praising children for attending must come after there is proof that the information has been processed. Therefore a child:

- can talk about what they have attended to
- can show work that indicates attention
- can role play what they have heard
- can follow directions they have heard
- can answer questions about what they have attended to

If a child has not learned then:

- a child has been distracted
- has found the time of information too long
- has only heard fragments of the information
- has no idea how to start the required task
- talks about irrelevant matters
- has difficulty answering questions
- annoys other children

Behaviour and Attentional Difficulties

The most important advantage to the attention given to ADDS is that it helped people to start to think about children who have difficulty attending. Like all 'syndromes' or in fact as with all learners, there are always levels of ability and different rates of learning. Attention difficulties are very similar yet there is variation from child to child. Some children go through phases of non-attention and some children have no idea how to attend perhaps because they have some brain damage or more simply have never been trained to attend. Children presenting learning difficulties which result from poor attention or classroom strategies will be noticed by teachers by the following behaviours;

- difficulty in prolonging spontaneous activities
- wander off when playing with other children
- cannot make choices and stick to them
- don't persist at work tasks set by adults
- easily distractible
- very restless and fidgety when adult is talking to a group
- find it hard to sit in seat
- misuse resources, pulling displays off walls, for example

Children who display these problems may also have:

- conduct disorder,
- an oppositional disorder,
- a mild form of Tourettes' syndrome,
- moderate to severe learning difficulties,
- difficulty with language (slight hearing losses),
- emotional and behavioural difficulties,
- or find certain areas of the curriculum more difficult

One can add children who find learning new tasks in maths difficult, children who have other problems on their minds such as difficulties at home, hyperactive children, anxious or attention-seeking children or a variety of other difficulties. Attentional difficulties rarely stand on their own.

When Do Adults Find It Most Difficult to Deal with the Problems?

When inattention is repetitive, annoying and spoils situations that the teacher has set up for all the class, then the adult may feel frustrated. When a teacher has to continually remind a child or remove the child and have to explain individually what the task is later whilst the other children are looking for help, again the adult can feel as if s/he is failing.

Most teachers in the main stream sector are usually unprepared for children who cannot attend. Teachers have usually organized their learning objectives and their resources and time in such a way that children who have characteristics that are difficult to fit into a plan are not perhaps given the encouragement that they need or in fact, the training they need to fit in.

Adults who find it hard to change their own behaviour to accommodate more complex behavioural difficulties in their classrooms do not help those children and in fact are more likely to exacerbate the problems. It often takes a lot of organization to manage the class in such a way that all of the children can receive training and skills in attending.

Quite often, adults may speak negatively and blame the children who do not fit and the difficulties the child has are reinforced by the school so that the child (or whole class) becomes 'known' and has a label to keep up to. What may have been solvable as an attentional problem becomes, possibly, more and more a long-term behavioural problem.

Ready to Be Receptive and for How Long?

Reverting to the horse guard or man in the box, I was told by an Information Officer that attention was due to training from the very first day of enlistment. When an officer yells 'eyes front', if the eyes don't respond the sergeant shouts, 'where are the eyes, soldier?' and the soldier replies, 'eyes front, sir'. So instruction, question and repetition. Old tricks die hard and in truth the over learning technique can never be disregarded.

There are reading schemes which do depend on children responding by looking and doing and repetition. Many teachers have organized these kinds of signs for use in the classroom. Some teachers put their hands in the air and without speaking have trained the children to show attention by copying the sign. By doing this a teacher tries to avoid the old 'pay attention' verbally, which then rises in volume as the children don't comply. However, the physical act, if accompanied by a verbal instruction, is sometimes easier for the child. 'Put pencils down' — by giving this instruction, the adult can see the results of attention and then can remind others to do the same. At this point, the volume of noise in the class will have halved, so asking children to look at something specific will halve the noise again, and like any gentle rolling stop, the adult will have less need to shout pay attention louder and louder. Although this may have a prescriptive feel about it, I would rather you looked at the training implications of it and worked out your own methods. You know that your aim is to get children to listen. For most children from day one, you have in your own head the method that you will use to get the children's attention. Suffice to know that these strategies in control and management are not part of training, and whilst some teachers prepare their subjects and resources, other teachers in the know map out their behavioural techniques and strategies to last over a year and think and resource the way in which they will see the year unfold.

Direction, information giving and instructions can only be useful if the children are attending and listening and looking exercises are crucial for the development of the 'good' class.

But words are very important because it is quite possible that the words of attention have not been learned by many of the children. So what are they? What words do you use?

Children have a variety of attention times. Some children can listen to very complex stories for long periods of time whether they see a picture or not, whilst others need to be rewarded by seeing pictures and by quick, easy to understand stories. How do you get the attention of both these groups without under-stimulating some and over-stimulating others (which may cause behavioural difficulties)? Some teachers look at children as they read, asking questions of some, speaking in the way characters speak, varying their voice throughout the story, make the story contingent on an activity that relates to the story, point out pictures and pick out interesting detail, make it a friendly session, an exciting session or just a relaxing session for enjoyment.

Knowing the attention spans for the children is directly to do with management and attention is directly to do with the next piece of practical work which follows and how well that supplements the attention. The work should also be seen to be the reward and be positive after the attention, so that it improves attention the next time. All strategies should work towards an improvement for the next time. Whilst attention is given, positive and social praise must be evidenced by all the children.

Differentiating for Attentional Ability

Start with the simpler book and decide that all the children will benefit from it. The more able group will enjoy the simplicity and colourful level of the story and if you sit the children so that the able sit next to the less able, the less attentive will have a model sitting next to them. Ask questions of the brighter pupil and immediately after that ask a slightly different question of the less able who will have received a cue from her or his neighbour. The reward is a look and a smile to encourage both children and return to the story. Work that supplements this for some children can be prepared ready, a more difficult story can then be read to the next group. This is one solution, others will think of different ways.

Improving Attentional Skills

Training attention for reading, especially with the slower readers, is part of those initial steps to reading. Recognizing the pattern for gaining reading skills helps to focus the adult's attention on what is needed in terms of learning behaviours:

- Training attention with physical and verbal prompts with social verbal praise. Children should repeat, consolidate and succeed.
- Improve the above training but reinforce group learning.
- Continue the approach but include blending, spelling tests that inspire early self confidence and the reading of simple sentences.
- Continue with more complex sentences and practice in reading aloud together and as individuals.
- Move to word building, give the child strategies to choose the correct letter as they move from left to right. Include repetition of irregular words. Repeat as often as necessary, children's attention improves if they know what comes next.
- Work with audio tapes and stories, the headphones will help the child to attend to the story. Oral and written comprehension.
- Child may now feel confident to work from books or cards, at grammar and comprehension.
- Attention grows, in various ways but it must be written into the scheme of teaching.

From Birth to Work — How Attentional Skills Are Nurtured

The simple way in which we train up this word starts when children are growing up. When babies are fed breast or bottle, they tend to gaze at the adult's face, a trusting gaze. They are usually rewarded by that adult speaking to them or returning the gaze. Mobiles and rattles are next. The rattle is like an intercom, the mobiles are like our sign, 'attention'. When the babies' eyes look at the mobile, look at the rattle, parents are training up early response behaviours. Eventually those items are replaced with words such as 'listen to me', 'look at me', 'listen and look'. Initially some enjoyment takes place after those words which reinforces the child to attention to attend.

Good parenting sometimes goes unnoticed because the children who do attend, learn and develop almost in spite of any conscious rewarding programme from parent or teacher. However, because of success the adult naturally gives positive responses. There is a danger that rewarding and encouraging appropriate learning behaviours is far more difficult than responding to the inappropriate behaviours and the slower work. And as mentioned before some children recognize this fact and may look to the inappropriate model to claim attention.

It is sometimes a surprise to teachers who clearly have had positive educational experiences to find that this doesn't all come naturally. For some young adults who have babies, the interest time is in the first year and as soon as language and motor skills show development, they find that this is the time that the child becomes 'in the way' and interest wanes. That is one reason; there are, of course, many others. Home behaviours that don't help the child to learn positive attention may be:

- parental neglect
- dependence on the dummy (dummy used to keep child quiet rather than as part-time pacifier)
- keeping the baby in a chair or pram
- television as the only stimulant
- keeping child in a cot in isolation
- talking to other adults and not to child
- finger foods, inconsistently through the day
- friend visiting, child in car seat
- annoyance at child requesting story when housework is more important
- smacking children who make noises

How does the teacher train up attention skills when the child's experiences are limited? In other words the parent has not modelled attention to the child or required the child to be attentive to the adult.

Showing attention does not mean a child is learning but a child needs to attend in order to learn. The following are three elements important to attention teaching:

1 Training up attention behaviour — make sure pupils know that good things get attention.
   - through games
   - through rules
   - through a variety of sounds or things

2 Directions — make sure children know what they are paying attention to

3 Practice — if the children's attention is not holding
   - what is the task?
   - how long is the task?
   - have you remembered to give attention before the attention of the child slips?

Conclusion

Putting innovations into practice is not just a matter of saying and doing. Like all developments it must be thought about, written down, rationalized, made practical, resourced, observed, managed and reflected upon. The best way to look at being actively involved in developing behaviours is to be very much part of your own system. It is best not to think of what you didn't do but to think about what you will do. There will be stumbling blocks to even the smallest of ideas but knowing that these are common does help. Changing your own approaches will often have a positive effect on many other aspects of the classroom. As an example, giving thought to gaining attention may change your approach to activities in your classroom. Training attention to task should be part of a process within the classroom and school.

7 Behaviour and Language

Introduction

I believe that it is important to have a wide knowledge of a child as well as the presenting condition. As explained in an earlier chapter, developing targeted behaviour programmes can go sadly wrong if only the presenting behaviour is relied on in making long-term decisions.

It is also important to raise a child's self esteem but this is only possible if you can work on the aspects of the child that s/he can see to be valid and successful. In the same way it is also important to recognize the symptoms of, for example, Attentional Deficit Disorder, but this should not be used as a blanket definition for all children who exhibit behavioural difficulties. One further explanation is discussed here and is equally valid.

Language and Parenting — Potential Problems at School

Many people have asked if children understand what adults are saying all the time. Good parenting involves early talking with the baby and toddler to build phonics, a sense of creating a naming vocabulary, playing with the child and using rules of play. Reasoning develops through this language pathway and understanding of social expectations can be internalized through play. However, it goes deeper than that, but the recognition of the building blocks goes some way to explaining why many children use challenging behaviours to express themselves. It is not unrealistic to assume language difficulties if we accept that most children with emotional and behavioural difficulties often present learning deficits in reading, spelling and writing. However, in education it is important to be aware of the inabilities and abilities of children to pick up useful language that they can assimilate and use to control their own behaviours and to help them to understand the required learning behaviour necessary in the classroom. More than awareness, a teacher must use language that the children can use consistently and understand to help in the management of behaviour in the classroom.

Children with emotional, behavioural and attentional difficulties may not initially have the language and therefore the reasoning capacity to understand social expectations. Their restricted language means that their inappropriate behaviour is a substitute for talk and they are unlikely to have the skills to internalize their own linguistic behavioural controls. Inability to express emotional or behavioural difficulties does not make the child a candidate for talk therapies. For many children with this problem, it means that the school environment is the best resource for exploring this area of difficulty. Increased adult awareness of the problems may relieve some of the possible rising difficulties the child may have in the classroom. With an awareness of language restrictions in children with behavioural problems, a teacher has other insights into ways to help the children to learn to control their own actions.

Whether you realize it or not, most children do not understand the meaning behind what most adults say to them. If they know the words, they quite frequently misinterpret them. Two examples are;

1   A teacher ran a lesson comparing the civilizations of the Greeks and the Tudors. With help and prompts, the children discussed the two. At the end, they were asked what civilization meant and they didn't know. Even with the context clues, the children were found to have forgotten what had been said in the lesson.

2   A teacher read a story to the children about a dog who was not obedient. The message from the story and the humour was based on the idea of obedience. Again, at the end of the story, the children had difficulty retelling the story and it was found that they had no concept of obedience.

Another interesting phrase that teachers often use is, 'You know what you are doing, so stop'. Without any clues about what he is presumed to be doing, the child then escalates a problem. The behaviour is then seen as manipulative and planned. Inferring that a child knows and can stop is not always a reasonable approach.

As children grow bigger, adults expect them to understand more. When the speaking gets faster and more complex, children are often baffled. Many react to what they think they understand which isn't always correct. Listening is also a fine art and if a child doesn't make sense of the words, then s/he stops listening and inattention follows. Learning is not taking place.

If rules are not very clear to a child very early on, it has a hard time understanding more complex rules as s/he grows bigger. Once the early part of learning is forsaken, the child is left in a more complex world with few reasoning skills and the expectation that he/she can manage.

Influence of Television and Computer Games

It is quite true that many aspects of modern life have interfered with children's normal language development. What about a controlled television viewing? We use it as a resource in schools. We ask questions and prepare follow up work. Children may learn to focus on and repeat information they have heard if the adult shows interest and allows conversation that stimulates the children.

However, misuse will mean that children will get into the habit of being able to watch and not assimilate and not talk back. A non-learning behaviour is growing from home.

- Television was created for information and entertainment. It nudged over the open fire and sits occupying the central spot in most living rooms. Families no longer look at each other, they look at the box.
- Television is said to increase conversation by acting as a stimulus, giving topics of conversation. Instead, it takes the *place* of conversation and is in reality a visual stimulation which is more momentary than long lasting.
- Some families no longer talk at the table over food. They sit watching television.
- Some families no longer play games in the evening, they watch television.
- Some families allow televisions in the bedrooms. Members of the family are now isolated and do not share the experience. Children may be visually stimulated with pictures that are not appropriate.
- Children may have used Saturday mornings to invent new games, draw or make things. They now watch adults shouting at them on children's television. Adults shout because they think children will respond better if they appear to be crazy. Perhaps teachers should follow suit?
- Talk is restricted to 'Did you like that?' or 'What's next?'
- Some adults think that if the child is watching television and is quiet, then it is best.
- For some television is not a learning process. In a learning process, information is gained and practised by the child through language. Most television programmes are only committed to short term memory.

In much the same way, the computers and game boys restrict social language. All these items are meant for individual use only. You may argue that they develop hand/eye co-ordination. You might also argue that the games can be shared to see who can score the most points. You may argue that some computer games are educational. They may be all these things, but if a child has not developed his own reasoning, then s/he will have difficulties in learning in school. A child will not be able to describe processes. The computers will do this for them rendering talk obsolete until a child enters a social environment (school) when personal learning skills and language needed to show ability, are called upon.

Bring Back the Board Game

To most children the board game will seem an anticlimax to the computer games. It doesn't do anything and you have to take turns and think out your moves. What does it do for language? It teaches social words. 'Pass the . . . please. It's your turn. . . . Can I have a go? What does the card say?' It is about being with two or more people. It is about co-operating and sharing. It teaches listening skills and attention skills. It is about facing people around a board and it promotes talking. Some adults in school have some time set aside in the classroom to play games. It is a legitimate and positive way to train up speaking and listening skills as in the National Curriculum.

Language and the Special School

A review in a special school is different from a report from a mainstream school. It is often far more detailed in terms of behavioural learning skills that are necessary for working within the National Curriculum. For most children with behavioural difficulties, the English curriculum causes a great deal of problems and especially the section on speaking and listening. The review looks at the child's strengths and weaknesses, which is useful for the following reasons; the strengths can be used to bolster the child's confidence, the strengths may also help areas in which the child is having difficulties, it helps the teacher to focus on what is next to teach the child and it helps the child's next teacher to continue the work of the previous teacher at a glance.

An example of this portion of the review may be as follows:

Speaking and Listening

Difficulties
L. has most difficulties in this section of the curriculum
L. cannot follow discussion in groups of more than three
L. is distracted by any movement or noise not within the general discussion
L. perseveres on one part of conversation and therefore isolates a meaning of his own from the original context
L. makes noises when in a large group which is listening to an adult or another child
L. puts up his hand to talk about unrelated subjects either to the discussion or to a direct question
L. puts up his hand but forgets why
L. needs to look at who is talking to focus on meaning
L. often forgets what previously known words are, 'What does it mean — barge?'
L. often forgets the subject of a conversation even when it is about himself. He says 'It doesn't matter to me.'
L.'s comments are always centred on the present
L. may often hear another child's news and take it on as his own, mixed with some of his own
L. is often bewildered by too much information

L. is confused by his difficulties and opts to get attention by being off task and out of group instead

L. finds it hard to take turns

L. finds it easier to draw his news than to write about it

Strengths

L. can speak for long periods of time when he is enjoying the topic

L. does enjoy one-to-one conversation

L. enjoys jokes with the group

L. enjoys more sociable activities in a group for short periods and related talk

L. can assimilate information if he focuses and consolidates it in many ways

L. works best when he blocks out other stimuli

L. can follow directions but will rely on prompts with three or more directions

L. enjoys talking about home and family with one adult

L. enjoys poems and songs

In the area of difficulties, there are many clues as to how to handle the problems L. presents us with. It also helps in other areas of the curriculum as well. L. clearly will manage better in a quiet group, with visual stimulus and small amounts of information which will need to be consolidated. In terms of language, he needs a great deal of focused talk making sure the information is in order.

Language and the Early Years

Language facility can be improved in the home but for many reasons it may get moved to the bottom of the agenda. Talking over a meal, planning an activity, reading a story together, all of these can come before clearing the house up. Too many times recently on a talk radio, I have heard mothers complaining that story reading means that the child has to sit on their laps and that during that time, they cannot be busy cleaning and therefore call the child a nuisance. The house can always be cleaned tomorrow but a child's day will never be repeated. Most parents no longer have the time to play with bricks, cars and boxes. They buy the items for the child but forget that they need to show them what to do. A parent must play and talk to the child in order to encourage independent play later. Children can only learn to internalize language if they have good play skills. What can school do to promote good language through play? Can a school take the time in the early years to replace the learning skills that home may have overlooked?

Being positive with language is hard. Children are faced with words that should never be used, but hear them all the time from the television, or when parents argue. They notice that the adult receives a lot of attention if they use a swear word. If the children copy the 'bad' words, they get a lot of adult attention, too.

We ask children to be positive in a world that abounds in negative language and experiences. Television is a prime example: the news is rarely good, situations in stories and cartoons occur because people have done or said the wrong things. People are encouraged to complain and the one who complains loudest gets the greatest attention.

Is it a surprise to any of us that children think that the more inappropriate the language, the louder it's said, the better it is at drawing attention? In our society doing the right thing is only honoured sometimes with awards on television, or the odd certificate. Rewards for good behaviour are rarer than the rewards for bad. It is so hard to say good things. Asked to describe their children, parents see that talk value is achieved by stating the 'bad' things and not the 'good' things. Teachers, thinking that they are positive, have been surprised at the observations taken in our centre that show that academic achievement gets some praise but negative reactions are much more in use than social positive reinforcement for on-task, sitting, helping, or otherwise co-operating in the classroom. How do we convince our children that it is more natural to do and say good things? How do we promote positive language and conversation? There are so many poor influences and a lack of positive influences that affect children.

For example, in one school, one assembly a week is given over to the children saying one good thing that they have done during the week. The words they must avoid are the easy ones, the 'avoidance' words; 'good', 'managed' or 'ignored other's behaviour'. These words are not acceptable because they don't get the child to think how they presented positive behaviour and also because they don't stimulate other words to express behavioural situations. Over time the children began to come up with forty totally different behaviours each week that were close to their own experiences, and could verbalize confidently what they had done.

Some children who enter reception class with a poor grasp of language may present you with the following problems;

- difficulty naming objects
- difficulty following simple directions
- difficulty in talking to other children
- difficulty understanding simple social signs
- an inability to categorize
- difficulty in understanding basic concepts and language used to extend learning
- restricted vocabulary

If a teacher recognizes these problems in a child, s/he needs to start at the developmental stage appropriate for that child and work on new concepts, cognition and language. The child will need to be talked through suitable behaviour, as well as being shown the correct physical response simultaneously. The child has to learn the language in order to internalize the directions.

In the Classrooms Teachers and Adults Must Remember

- To make eye contact with children when they speak to them. Too often teachers don't look at children because they learn to direct their talk to everyone and there are so many children in each class. Eye contact is hard when you are always trying to cover so much.

- Use simple directions for children initially. Get children to repeat any instructions or complex information. If it is easier draw a picture on the board, or write it simply so that most children can read it. In some classes this is not always necessary, but a few children may be missing out. You can tell who it is by their behaviour. Make sure you don't isolate them by picking on them, but get someone close to repeat it, someone the child may look up to, or place the children where they can visually be reminded about the direction with hints from their peers.

- Treat new words with respect. Make sure children know what they mean. It is all very well to stretch children by using a less restricted vocabulary but remember the ones who are not gaining from it. They will tell you. Look at their behaviour, do they all understand you?

- If children are running around the classroom and you are asking them to stop because they are disruptive, they will not hear you. You will have to stop them before they can understand what you want to say. If they are excitable, sit them down near you and wait for them to settle. A child who has been on the go will not be ready for a talk from a cross adult. They need to tell you what it is they are supposed to be doing.

- Bring a story to life when you read a story. Ask the children stimulating questions. Talk to children about 'what happened' or 'what if.'

- Give the children a language to learn not only in the classroom but in the school. Use assemblies to bring the children together with a language that binds them. Examples of this language may be — to manage, knowing what to do in my head, looking after my hands and feet, ignoring other children's behaviour, helping other children listening to reading in pairs. Build up situations where accepted or desired behaviour becomes part of the children's way of expressing appropriate behaviour. For example, 'We do not run when walking through the hall' to 'I will walk through the hall'.

- Do not give swearing any attention at all. It is old advice but it is the right advice. If you react, you are telling the child that it is a valid means of communication. It is valid, we all use those words, they are in the dictionary but they need to have a place. The most important factor is that the child does not have enough words and the best defence is to train up new words, expand a child's experience with words, and give the child a chance to use them and to get responses for them and to praise them for acquiring those interesting words. It takes time, but you are not trying to change a child's responses to the world from their own world overnight.

Conclusion

The important factors involving behaviour and language are not that children do not understand or misinterpret what we say, although we must be aware of these problems, but that children need to learn new ways of talking and internalizing talk that they may have missed out on in their early years. It is a difficult task and one that needs to be incorporated into any behavioural programme or in training up of learning skills within the classroom setting. The task of managing the behaviour of learners is a challenge of enormous complexity. Anna Freud called attention to the importance in analysis of teacher and parent behaviour and all those other factors in the child's natural habitat. Teaching and learning are within many realms and all of them appreciate the exploration of the behaviours of all involved in education. There will never be a consistency in the backgrounds of children or adults, but a consistency of communication would make the task of educating a sharing and developing one.

8 Pre-school Behaviour Management Needs

Introduction

The most important early social training ground, next to the family, is the pre-school experience. It is possibly the first time that many children will learn how to share. I remember my child on his first day in pre-school. He snatched a spade from another child in the sandpit. I was about to intervene when the nursery nurse motioned me to stop. Another slightly older child quietly leaned forward, took the spade from my child and replaced it with his own. He said, 'You can borrow mine and we'll take turns.' My child and I were both amazed by this kindness. My child seemed to learn quietly from his peer without any problems. Perhaps this is an isolated happening in my own child's development but in the best possible world it stands to show how from small beginnings great things can be learnt. My child continues to enjoy sharing.

Nursery Schooling

Many pre-school teachers and nursery nurses who have been observing the early years closely for long periods often have the ability and sensitivity to recognize rising behavioural difficulties.

Box 9:   Importance of observation

My mother was a teacher and nurse in pre-school for twenty-five years. During that time she kept careful records and observations, descriptions of children aged between two and five. These were detailed, sometimes humorous, with the children's personalities and characters captured as if in small miniatures. She used them to share with parents all the trials and tribulations of the early social and academic adventures. What has always interested me as I reread the pages, is the extraordinary way in which the actions and language give strong indications of what the children need in terms of early intervention that may help them to cope more easily as they develop toward school years. In fact, the final comments include intuitive ways in which to avert problems or to work on strengths within the next year of nursery. Because of this reportage and the years of

---

watching my mother's work and approach to young children, I recognize the importance of using that experience of people working within the early years and their ability to influence the learning skills that are needed for successful and socially rewarding school years.

Nursery teachers, therefore, have the advantage of being in at the very start of the socializing process, sharing the early influences and experiences of the young family. Initial factors that are important for the future are;

- the child's attitude to entering nursery
- the parents' attitude to the child entering nursery
- the child's ability to play, or ability to learn to play
- the child's ability to share, or ability to learn to share
- the child's ability to listen, or ability to look and listen

These pre-entry skills can be carefully observed by the staff. If a toddler is entering at the age of two-and-a-half, then there are two-and-a-half years in which to get these initial factors right or help them to be right and then to continue with the kinds of activities within nursery that train up more particular learning skills through play. Nursery school is replicated and rehearsed in the rest of life.

The Child's Attitude to Entering Nursery

Teachers of pre-school children need to observe closely the behaviour of the new entrants to nursery school.

- after the initial shock of losing their mother, is the child captivated by a toy, or other activities that absorb his/her attention? or
- does the child cry and sit, withdrawn, unable to focus on one object or person?
- does the child throw the toy to one side and kick the nearest person?
- does the child accept drink or a biscuit, or reject it and throw it on the floor?
- does this behaviour continue over ten days?

There are many other signs, but how does a teacher or nursery nurse get past the difficulties and change the toddler's attitude to a more positive approach? It may be that the toddler has not had the early interaction with the parent in naming and being shown how to use a toy. S/he may not have had tickles and early rules, maybe no quiet times looking at pictures with an adult, learning the value of early contacts. Perhaps an early activity as simple as making eye contact and playing 'peep-bo' is called for. If a toy is thrown, it needs to be returned, it needs to be given a value and a place. Five minutes' training every twenty minutes may cover a great deal and start to change a toddler's attitude to nursery.

The Parents' Attitude to the Child Entering Nursery

Many parents are either sending the child to the nursery and running off to work with some relief, or sending the child reluctantly because they must go off to work or have been advised that it would be best for the child to play with others because s/he is an only child. Maybe they want to have more stimulation for the child than they can offer at home in terms of play experience. The entering of nursery or reception classes at four-and-a-half either consolidates behaviours that the child has been developing at home or presents the child with situations with which s/he is ill equipped to deal with. It may be the time that parents are first introduced to direct criticism either of the child's behaviour or indirectly become aware of failing in the way in which they have managed their child. Four-and-a-half is crunch time, the time when children enter the realm of a new social world with new expectations. Children can be prepared in the home for this or not. It is the time when children with poor socializing skills can worsen because of other parental, teacher/nursery nurse and peer attitudes to negative behaviours. Hopefully, the other adults will sympathize and work positively with the child and parents. Young children who 'do' the right things are further rewarded by positive attentions and continue on the positive route, young children who 'do' the wrong things learn quickly the negative attentions that sustain the negative behaviours. Parents who show a willingness to work with the school, are often rewarded by teacher attention and a willingness for adults to work alongside their child. Parents who have difficulty understanding the consequences of early learning, often blame the school and prolong the negative attitudes to school to the child at home.

The Child's Ability to Play, or Ability to Learn to Play

Many factors must be in place before playing can be learnt. A child may have the ability to play but has not had the experience of using the ability to focus his or her play. The adults may have been good at talking to the child and including the child in more adult activities. However, many parents think that taking out the child, having more physical encounters, tickling, ball play, watching television and including the child in adult conversation is the extent of their intervention. They are right, in that the child has the language ability but may be ready to play independently, and needs the nursery to develop those skills further. Those parents may possibly be open to being involved in a more focused way and to provide the environment at home in which the child can practise nursery skills.

Children who have minimal language but show a propensity to develop their language using the play situations and toys in nursery need a similar but slightly different approach. Whereas one child needs to internalize his language by a new independent involvement in what s/he is doing, another may need to talk more openly while he is playing, prompted by the adult. Whilst these differences are subtle, it should be noted that the behavioural responses by the adult are part of the child's development toward a happy introduction into the more formalized setting of school.

The Child's Ability to Share, or Ability to Learn to Share

Sharing and co-operating are both crucial to a successful schooling. Clearly it has implications for language development but it also has implications for taking and carrying out directions willingly, listening to adults and peers, being able to manage and control behaviour as part of a group, taking responsibility for helping others and being able to share ideas and the making of projects. Teachers and nursery nurses need to encourage children by having times in the day in which activities can take place that contain the language of sharing and the practical experience of sharing work together. Particular to sharing is being able to listen to stories and take turns in asking questions. Listening to other children talking and commenting is hard but a good skill for children to learn. At this stage, the adult must encourage good listening as it becomes more vital to learning in the more formal atmosphere of the primary school. The adult models responses to children's talk. If children can master the art, it is easy to see that they have been able to listen, to consider and to respond appropriately.

The Child's Ability to Listen, or Ability to Look and Listen

Sitting still and listening for periods of time is always hard and there are always some children who cannot attend that early. These children must sit in the front as they are quickly distracted and seem to have little comprehension of how to be interested in a story or just 'talk'. Teachers/nursery nurses must slow their talking down, get eye contact and try to give those children positive attention rather than negative prompts. It is a difficult skill, because already there must be a balance between training what is not acceptable with training what is acceptable and children learn best when they have positive feedback.

Being Alert to Difficulties

Setting boundaries early, giving children ways in which to practise simple house rules, asking children to repeat rules so that they internalize them is a good start for many children who have not had those experiences. Being firm on important matters gives the children an understanding of the difference between serious and fun, things that matter and those that are more light hearted. Nursery can teach children respect for learning early and a desire to do more and learn more. It is the place where all the important skills and strategies to acquiring a good education are founded. It is a great responsibility, and having an awareness and a continuing consciousness about the training of learning behaviours is essential in the early learning centres. It is not so much what you do but how you do it, why you do it and who you do it with. Children can play with adults as well as children and the adults must recognize that modelling play behaviour is as important as teaching table skills.

Early Identification of Problem Behaviour

Quite often some of those children with the more difficult behaviours can be identified early enough for adults to work consistently with the child in preparation for school. In some cases, the child can move through nursery and only present more identifiable characteristics of a syndrome or category in the primary school. Aggressive behaviours in young children only become more apparent when the child becomes bigger whereas previously the adults may have just picked up the pieces and felt the toddler would grow out of it. Children who bully early on need to have special help. The nursery can have several options and work over the period of the child's stay. All activities during the day from sand pit work to eating at the table can foster a responsibility toward peers and a language that can control the aggression and stimulate new words for good relationships. Parents who have difficulty with their children should be encouraged early to come into the nursery and to work with the adults in charge on programmes that can easily work within the home, too. These parents need to see that educational institutions are friendly, are not opposed to helping their child/ren and will encourage receiving schools to continue remedial help.

While it must be appreciated that the two- to five-year-olds grow from their ego stage into group play over time and their cognitive understanding is emerging through the period, it is important to use that knowledge and make use of it.

Activities that Teach Behavioural Skills and Strategies

This type of motivation and training should exist from the beginning up so that the team through many years consists of parents, nursery nurses, teachers, classroom assistant, managers. The development of training behaviours should include:

- mouthing and touching,
- skills of partnerships,
- group co-operation,
- sharing,
- listening,
- looking,
- attending,
- sitting,
- respecting property,
- following directions,
- showing work,
- confidence and self esteem,
- dependent learning,
- independent learning,
- understanding of what is good and what is not,
- understanding rules,
- respecting others.

All those common learning behaviours involved with a growing child should be seen as common aims through school for individuals and groups.

Arrival — Making sure that toddlers have a positive entrance into school, with welcoming and confident words, is essential to recognizing that school is a good place. The child can immediately recognize that s/he belongs to this place and knows where his/her permanent peg is to hang a coat. It is everyone's right to feel that education belongs to all. What happens next is important, the sense of knowing what to do helps the child to start the day. An early direction, an invitation to join in, and help to choose means to the child that the adult here will help, listen and be a resource for the future.

Choice — being confident of what to do means choices can be made. By this time, a child has been helped to experience a range of activities and to formulate ideas about favourite activities. Asking questions about activities, listening to ideas about them and sharing with others are exercises for the future. The adult is still quite controlling but the child is being helped to take on independent decisions.

Using the right language to do this is important:

- what will you choose?
- how will you do it?
- why is it your best choice? and
- who would you like to do it with?

Free play — After practising choice with the adult, the child can handle free play with a few rules in hand: ways to get on with people, sharing, being careful not to hurt each other, looking after those who need it, talking through the activity, taking other's ideas and having fun.

Creative play — The skills required to use lots of resources to make and paint involve all the above processes. But it also means that a child needs encouragement from the adult, a lot of social praise, a lot of showing a work, some ideas to think about and discussion about sharing of resources. The situation can be so good that attention can be focused and concentration can develop. Children who wander can do so, but in the long term it would be helpful to ask children to finish most work and to be praised. They also need to be sure what they are being praised for, not just the picture, but for sharing paints, helping to clear up and showing concentration and a good attitude to work. Praising 'how' a task was completed means that the good behaviour is likely to be repeated and the ability to behave well will increase.

Story time — Sharing a story means that the adult is getting the attention. It also means that several children will have to share giving the adult attention and listening and then sharing the experience. Learning to enjoy an experience together and perhaps repeating it over and over, means that you soon get used to group learning. Remember that children and adults like to hear what they know. It makes them feel confident and ready to learn the next thing. This exercise is just as likely to improve group learning as sharing the table at creative time or eating together at lunch time.

Snack/lunch time — Some children may not know how to sit at table and for some it's a brand new adventure, for others it is frightening and makes eating hard, while for many it is an everyday occurrence. Learning social rules is good when you are small: listening to what others have to say, asking people to pass things to you, eating with the proper utensils, talking quietly, and asking about the food that is being eaten, having a joke and feeling important and part of a social occasion. Behaviour that is co-operative is important, it helps all early learning.

Outdoor play — It involves children becoming used to a lot of space in which to play and interact with others, as well as learning to listen to the adults who are guiding this new learning experience. This is very important preparation for playtime and gym time when you get to the big school.

Imaginary play — A creative form of play where children are using all the early language which is basic to future success. But imaginary play does not just happen. Children need to be helped to extend their vocabulary and to master it to such a degree that it can be internalized so that they can control their own play world. Imaginary play means working things out and reasoning out situations.

Home time — The end of the school day which involves clearing up and collecting one's belongings, helps to teach the child to organize his/her own possessions, and is a time when small rituals sign off another day, hopefully leaving the children looking forward to the next day at school.

It is important to share all the good things with parents at this time, they need to know what is important and how they can help their child. For some parents coming into nursery and observing others working with their child, the experience can often stimulate them into ways of working at home. Many people find it hard to remember those very early years. They may remember circumstances but not what they did. We move on from our early play and because we concentrate on our next activities, we take with us only the skills we learnt through the toys but not so often memories of the toys themselves.

Box 10:   First days in school

I remember my first behaviour in a nursery school. I placed my heels firmly in the gravel and it took three adults to pull me, gravel spitting upward, through the door. I see that experience like a photograph, some other person but not me. I never entered another school dramatically quite like that and reflecting I can find no explanation in my own head for my behaviour. One thing I do consider is that all through that particular school, I seemed to exist only in my own head, I see myself lying on a mat at sleep time wondering at the multi-petticoats above me, I remember the pride I felt when I was entrusted with returning an umbrella to my teacher kindly lent to my mother and I remember realizing in the bus that I had forgotten my knickers and having to go into a shop to buy a pair and slip them on behind a potted plant. Such is what early pre-school memories are about. I must have learnt so many other skills that prepared me for a lifetime of school because I have spent so long in those halls of education.

Conclusion

All these areas, and many more, train up behaviours that children need in order to learn. For those children who find all or any of these steps difficult, it is important to start where they are and work toward the acquisition of the initial steps to learning behaviours. Difficulties are always quickly spotted but remediating them is often a longer process. However, pre-school is the environment in which the child is first introduced to the complex world of education outside the home. There are of course other situations, visits to friends and relatives, going to the dentists and the doctors, using different kinds of transport, to shows, museums, swimming pools. All these places are training grounds for social behaviours, good and bad and for the consolidation of skills learnt in the home or pre-school. It is a very busy time for learning social skills and an adult needs to control these initial experiences so that the child finds them meaningful, not confusing or frightening. By reception class, children have many behaviours they have learnt over five years and for some, those behaviours may make their first school years very difficult for teachers and peers alike.

9 Play, Playtimes and Behaviour

Introduction

I had been to nine schools by the time I was twelve. In each school, I had to rearrange my thoughts, my friends, my activities and my place in the new area. Each new place was beset by its own traumas for me, quietly assimilated and quietly overcome. At six I found myself high in the Alps for the summer with my sisters. We spoke only a little French, enough to communicate. We would play a game of sardines. One night, we were playing and for the first time I was the child to go and hide first. I ran down the mountainside, and hid under a bush, excited and pleased to find such a good, so far unused, hiding place. I sat there for a long time. I watched the sun playing on the top of Mont Blanc and the goats moving around on the mountainside below. The sun slowly disappeared and the slightly cooler evening set in. I didn't move, just in case. They had all forgotten me. I waited and waited until torch lights appeared and people called me. They found me, a little stiff but none the worse for wear. The adults were kind but they couldn't make up the disappointment that welled up inside me and that I remembered for ever. Play is important to children and gives them memories that can stay with them forever.

Box 11: Terrors of playtime when you are 'new'

Starting in a new school in Richmond when I was seven meant that dreadful playtime when there was no friendly face or known adult. Everyone else seemed to have partners to play with, kiss chase in those dreadful open toilets, to play marbles clustered around the drains, to play 'two balls' along every available wall space, to play film stars, running to wall and back with names that may start with DD, Donald Duck or Diana Dors, hopscotch and all those myriad of games that children used to play in the playground. I walked out looking at everyone and trying to find a wall space to lean up against when I bumped into a small boy. I picked him up, said sorry and continued on my way to lean against the wall. A large boy sauntered over, he headed straight for me, I smiled, he punched me hard in the stomach said, 'that's for hitting my brother' and strolled off, leaving me blinking the tears away and trying not to look upset in alien territory.

A child's perception of playtime is very different from that of an adult. Adults may see the time as non-specific, time for a rest from the children or to prepare lessons, but it may be that playtimes are the times that children most need adult support.

Improving Playtimes

I asked adults on a course to remember games they had played, and friends they had played with. All save one, remembered as if yesterday, the details of time in the playground. When asked to remember time in class, it was more difficult. Strange that for the adults, playtimes and lunch play are a momentary bother, a sigh of relief when all the children are turned over to the mid-day assistants. In fact the ratio of children to adult tends to rise on these occasions. Playtimes can either run smoothly or be the worst time of the day for incidents. Rather like the island in *Lord of the Flies*, the untrained and unsupervised playground can lead to endless battle. The poorest of social skills can be practised in early school playtime ranging up to those difficult secondary breaks. Adults will look at the children and do endless observations on playground bullying and respond to the bullying but preventative measures that mean a hard look at adult resource is the last consideration. Improved playtimes mean time and energy and initial adult direction in primary and junior playgrounds. This time used well can improve classroom attention and co-operation and should be prepared as all other times on the curriculum. During most courses for staff in school, the focus for problems is usually the playground and yet the teachers feel divorced from this time. A school recognizes the problem but no-one feels that the problem is theirs to solve. However, taking the problem into the open, most teachers agree that if they spent time training up good playground behaviours, then in the long term, it would be time well spent. As we discussed earlier, it does mean that adults have to change their behaviour and to motivate themselves by being interested in not only improving the school but also children's behaviour when they return to class after a good play. One school had taken steps by using their year 6 as a work force. The children would take one game onto the playground each to organize with a group of the younger years. Adult input was in supporting the year 6 and suggesting ways in which they could encourage the children around them to play. A good playtime can help children to train up social and learning behaviours and should be a vibrant part of all school scheduling. Most schools solve the problem of bad plays by cancelling them, preferring to give the children less time to play when they are not controlled. In fact, play should be lengthened and encouraged as an important school activity for encouraging future skills.

Different kinds of behavioural skills can be trained up in certain play activities. For example;

- Team ball games train up children's ability to stay with a situation, to practice self control, to be aware of other's input and to be encouraging as well as working hard at one's own input. The games also show children how to release personal wishes for a common purpose. It shows children how to talk to and share with team mates, to control gross motor skills and to cooperate. A teacher can improve all skills by encouraging good sportsmanship and making expectations clear, by playing with the children as a model and praising good team work.
- Fantasy play and make believe can develop language, stimulate energy and capacity to learn, practise and consolidate old skills and to help puzzle out new situations and experiences. It also helps children to combat the feeling of helplessness in the adult world by fulfilling that wish to grow up. Others can be included in the game and growth can be together. The adult should promote a safe environment and provide resources necessary to make the play important.

There are many more examples because play can help a child to experiment with the world around him/her. It can stimulate creative activity, encourage imagination and fantasy, develop social skills, physical and mental abilities and give skills for construction. Within all these areas learning behaviour is entwined in all these experiences. Attention to the activity, sharing, listening, preparing, resourcing, talking, managing, concentrating are all good learning words incorporated in the activity of play that should be encouraged in all schools through to secondary placement. Even more important, the early skills should lead to less problematic times in the older years when free time becomes even more onerous for some children.

Play Behaviour is Always Important

Play is about the child and his/her continual interaction with the world that will last for its whole life. Acquiring pre-school behavioural skills related to learning has been discussed in the previous chapter. Once early social skills are developed, they too can grow and be built upon throughout early schooling. Play develops cognitive understandings in children and also self-discipline. An active involvement in playtimes will only be seen by the outcome and by long-term adult support to playtime policies just as with a classtime curriculum. Play is often repetitive. A child loves that, while adults take fleeting pleasure in repetition and assume that children will be bored by it. The adult can fall off-task quicker than the child when occupied by playing, but the better mastered a play activity, the more pleasure a child receives. As teacher, you may not be able to change the world but you may have more awareness of the playtime as important to you in the classroom, and to prepare the children as you might any other time of the day.

Play should:

- stimulate creative activity
- promote social skills (making friends, develop personal and group responsibility, co-operation and the ability to ask for help)
- build up physical and mental abilities
- encourage the use of fine motor skills (construction and building)
- develop language.

Young Children's Play

Of course, every play situation or toy develops various skills. If you remember, children's toys develop with the child. In other words, first toys —

- do something by touch, are easy to hold
- when you do something, something else happens
- one action must be followed by another to make something else happen and so on.

Colours, shapes and use grow more complex from the simple, to help the child into an increasingly complex world. We still need the toys and the play, technology will never replace the early experiences, although it has a place when the child is ready. When a child enters school, he or she enters a new play situation with lots of unfamiliar children, not many comforting adults, fewer if no toys, marks on the playground, perhaps larger apparatus. If the child has had a good reception class, the teacher may have prepared the children with ideas for imaginative play or taught playground games. S/he may ask each child to talk about what they will do at play or who they have planned to share their game with. Only by making the teacher's interest part of the routine, will play have real meaning in today's school. Many problems begin at this time.

Most psychotherapists involved in play base their approach on the recognition that young children are limited in their ability to communicate problems like adults. However, poor playground skills demonstrate problems and children are communicating their difficulty in understanding a social situation. They often cannot work out the conflicts without adult support. They look to adults to solve their behaviours. If the adults are not there and punish poor play instead of training it up, then the problems are not solved, they are exacerbated.

If we simplify Freud's idea that play is motivated behaviour and that it is caused by the child's feelings and emotions, conscious and unconscious, then it would seem that we need to sustain and encourage what is, essentially, a tool waiting to be used. Play doesn't stop in school. It should be actively pursued by adults recognizing the process of developing and maturing within the 'play' definition. Other tools to extending play might be curiosity, exploration and manipulation. After all the idea of hide 'n seek supposedly is part of our heritage as the stalker and the prey.

Play therapists note that children play to recreate pleasurable happenings or thoughts with objects around him/her. If a child repeats unpleasant happenings enough, he or she becomes inured to them, relieving some of the pressures. The child then feels less of a passive and helpless victim. If we agree the premise then perhaps it is the adults who do not encourage developing play techniques that are in turn developing children's ways of coping. After all the importance of adult approval is basic to children's motivation to learn from the adult in the classroom.

If a child lacks play experiences and situations then the adult needs to give the child a new way of expressing him or herself, even to him or herself. It is important to note significant play behaviour in reports and to use the information when developing programmes for children.

Play can be thoroughly enjoyable, fun and satisfying for the child. It can exist for its own sake and which practises skills and abilities that develop perceptions, fine motor and other skills necessary in the stages of development.

Problems at Playtimes

A lot of children find playing at playtimes difficult, after all not all children have had those early positive experiences with involved and active parental guidance. Sharing and talking to friends and having particular skills in age appropriate games for the playground is not something that every child can do. Children in this situation look for those other ways of communicating which are not right and which lead to conflict in the playground. When others don't understand their particular interests and don't respond, fights start. When they cannot share their own world they make an impact on the world in the only ways that they can to get attention and notoriety.

Social difficulties can arise but with adult intervention children can struggle to find those previous strategies in their heads and to reconcile them to present expectations. Children who cannot do that will have to depend on late tuition. You can understand this better when you hear that it takes five years for a child to co-ordinate all the facts and practice in learning to read. A child who has not been able to do this has to learn later and when s/he does not manage to learn within a year, teachers and adults feel frustrated and incompetent. If a first year teacher recognizes the difficulties and passes on the reading development of the child to the next two years then a realistic expectation can be met. The same strategies fit social play and behavioural skills. Adults must be as actively involved in a long-term commitment to teaching learning and behavioural skills as they are to the teaching of reading.

Classroom activities can enhance children's abilities to manage playtimes. Board games, construction games, building games, walks to local parks are all experiences that build up sociability and co-operation. Time spent on these activities can help the children to manage the curriculum with more patience and understanding.

Historically, children used to play to train up skills for adult life. The young Indians made bows and arrows, and rode horses as soon as they could sit up. They helped make food or catch it. If computers are our future then it follows that our children should be playing with them early. However, we are more complex than this. We do not have only one area of the world to enter, our choices are many. We need to be taught the ability to make choices and to reason for ourselves. To do this we still need to go through the stages of development necessary for good learning. In a sense we need a more stimu- lating and more aware childhood than previously. Instead of more television as children to prepare us for a media future, we need more reading and more independent play to develop our brains to match the complexity of the electronic world. Our complex world has given parents the wrong messages, children don't need 'things' and less involvement, they need a more active involvement and help to be independent with all the 'things'. A good playtime can improve attention to tasks, stimulate interests, train up social skills, improve language, improve sportsmanship, build confidence and reasoning, cement good relation- ships and help the body relax into more controlled learning environments.

Conclusion

A good teacher values the playtime and has an input into it. S/he makes sure that all the children have a good idea of what they will play outside or at least have the equipment to play. Even if it means no long coffee break, a teacher might like to help a child who has difficulty into the playground on a pro- gramme that includes a good play with adult help. Initial work of this kind can have pay offs at the expense of a few cups of coffee. If you usually use the playtime for preparation, choose an activity which the children can help to prepare. Children get a lot from adults who help at playtimes and respect adults who respect their play.

10 Action Research and Behaviour

Introduction

The staffroom is a hive of conversation at times, a place of refuge, of con-solation, and preparation. A teacher's day is spent moving over the classroom, through corridors, out to the playground, to the resource rooms and snatching moments to organize activities, outings and action in the classroom, writing reports and managing and teaching children. If anyone had ever said to me that I might be involved in action research simultaneously, I might have looked at them in disbelief. On reflection however, it may have been the suggestion that focuses all these activities on the major element of a teaching life and that is being a *thinking teacher*. In a sense the school is the shop floor of early life, it is the place where all our understandings come together and in which children's behaviour and attitudes for the future are formed. It is also the place in which what we do is important and essential and should be good practice. It is also the best place to find out what is working and what is not working in education, in what is taught, in resourcing teaching, in learning behaviour and teaching behaviour. It can also be a place of sharing. Action research opens classrooms and helps teachers to understand that they are not islands within a sea but all part of one land mass, where communication, assistance and co-operation between adults can do more for the children in a school than a closed classroom that begs criticism and defence. Behaviour is always high on the agenda and it often is a sensitive area. Making the subject an open and on-going positive communication among staff can be helped by making it also part of an action research which can develop staff, focus on the children and improve school practice.

Action Research

Action research was initiated by Kurt Lewin in 1946 (see Kemmis 1980) who viewed action research as a spiral of circles involving identifying a general idea, reconnaissance, general planning, developing an action step, implementing the action step, then evaluating and revising the plan. And again, one spirals into the next action step and a revision of the general plan. In a sense action research could be a never ending story as an exploration into the changing nature of education.

John Elliot has been the modern mover of the idea of action research. His initial interaction with action research was concerned with school curriculum reforms which should still hold an important place with the practising main stream teacher. More recently, there has been a movement to place action research more firmly within the higher education sector. Action research can be successfully initiated from the academic cloisters in which case the researchers are there to facilitate 'insider research' in schools without fostering dependence on them. In this case the practitioner can concentrate on the activity of research and have the facility to share and relieve some of the burden of analysis. The payoff for the school establishment is often high, that is if all staff feel good and not resentful of intrusion.

However, my interest is in having action research back where I believe it belongs, within the school, the classroom or unit. I believe that its strength is in its ability to develop the school with ideas and formulated practice for investigating or extending curriculum, teacher practice or behavioural policies within the school. I feel that it can contribute to the professionalism of teachers in schools. I also feel that teachers need a more professionally based training that includes understanding what behaviours children need to have before they can approach the National Curriculum, and how to make the classroom into a continually developing environment growing and developing new dimensions.

Teachers should be aware of aspects that keep teaching alive, exploring issues in teaching within the school. Just as modernism was the artists' escape from the restrictions of representational painting, negating the end product to celebrate the means, so we need to look at teaching in terms of what we are doing. That we are not just recreating what we believe teaching to be but that we understand and advertise the essential important ingredients in the art of teaching children to learn. In the spirit of this, it may also be important to introduce action research as an aspect of initial teacher training as a catalyst to extending teacher interests and professionalism.

What I would like to interest educators in, is the positive continuation of active research and involvement in and development of teachers, their practice or classroom management, and of their unit or school in which they are involved. It is not just the case of having an idea and putting it into practice such as Co-operative Play or Circle Time, *it is the continuing reflection and improvement of the practice that is important.* For instance, an example of ongoing action research is built into Co-operative Play as it develops the practice of new and long serving staff, school practice, visitors, students and parents. Because observation and discussion and reflection take part in its structure, it is part of a continual investigation into how to improve practice.

Reflection

All teachers need their own mini-action research and most teachers do albeit unconsciously. However, these efforts tend to be short-lived and can increase frustration in the classroom. A teacher might consider a certain action with a child, find that it doesn't work, lose the recording sheet under other piles of paper, give up and carry on with the next activity. There needs to be a method and it needs to be on-going and for that some planning is necessary. It also needs to be shared because often reflection and ideas can come in discussion and can also help long-term motivation.

You might even notice small ideas or positive situations developing that might be important to future plans. Reflection is about looking at your own behaviour or others' behaviour and finding ways of improving or initiating practice. It is my experience that reflection is often difficult for students and newly qualified teachers as it requires a certain amount of understanding and experience about long-term planning. There is also a difficulty in recognizing that reflection can give ideas for personal and classroom development and is not just a way to find areas for others to criticize. If you implement a plan, make sure that you are consistent but that you are also planning the next move, implementing it, evaluating what you have done and reflecting on its development.

We find that staff are very interested in certain aspects of the school. It may be that they want to add something, or question something, or just want to be part of it in a contributory fashion. Action Research involves everyone in the school at some level, or just one or two people. Whatever, it focuses interest into the school and raises staff awareness of the many facets of teaching and development. Should an aspect of the school need a focus, staff can be encouraged to study the problem long-term, make changes, put them into practice, reflect on how they work, make further changes and put them into practice.

In the end there should be a greater awareness of a collegiate approach to managing the idea of behaviour from greater awareness of a stimulated, considering staff. Exclusions happen when the child's problems overcome any forward planning by all staff to consistently help the child within the framework of the school. This may be an ideal area to stimulate action research. The time spent in sharing will be rewarded. A way to start may be for two staff to form a working party and slowly disseminate ideas, letting plans grow day by day. Some staff may be more adept at creative planning whilst all members may be keen to apply the plan. Talk to other staff and put all the ideas together. Create a structure and make sure that it is supported.

The aim of action research is the improvement of practice including gains in understanding and changes in action. It is part of our professional practice which is under exploration with improvement in mind. Improving the practice of being an action researcher includes; the gathering of evidence, a personal side, collaboration with others, discussion with colleagues. Rather than the application of rule of one's findings, it is reflection on one's learning experience which leads to change.

Figure 10.1 shows the way in which a whole school might participate in an ongoing research. This implies a far greater organization and motivation by the staff. However, once co-ordinated can be an exciting prospect for a school and its professionalism.

Figure 10.1: *Whole school research*

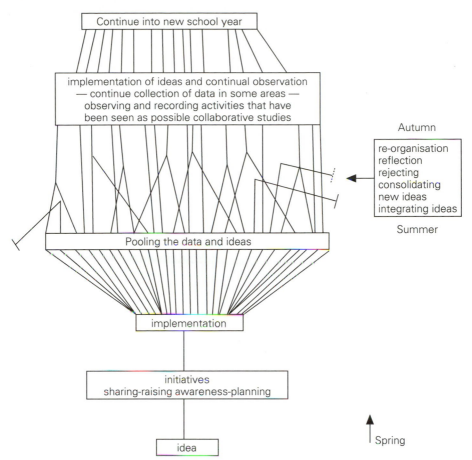

Projected long term development of strands of research in one establishment

At a school, there is always a mixture of staff, with a variety of experiences and motivations, reasons for being there and different levels of interest in what they do. Any whole school research may start out with interest and committment but there will always be a certain amount of fall off. Growth of the research has to take it to account a continual revision of the situation, reflection and the development of new ideas. It needs always monitoring by an overall researcher who can motivate and rebuild in order to keep the thread of the research together.

Conclusion

Action Research is the study of a social situation with a view to improving the quality of action within it. Action research aims to improve practice rather than

to produce knowledge. Action research theories are validated through practice. The values are about the quality of practice and not just outcomes. The
control of the research lies with the insider as researcher rather than an outside
professional researcher. The concerns are related to the everyday practical
problems experienced within the school or organization. It is the point of view
of those involved that is important. To start you need to isolate a general issue
for research, then look at all the facts, and test out your ideas.

You might look at the references in the bibliography or consider joining
CARN the Collaborative Action Research Network, Email: OHANLONC@BHAM.
AC.UK.

11 Practice and Policy

Introduction

Convincing others of your ability is a difficult part of any training process or in fact any situation in which you are under observation. You cannot stop every few minutes to give someone a reason for what or how you are doing something. When a student teacher is having 'in-class' experience, a lot of the realities of teaching begin to arise.

Box 12: A testing experience

For example, when taking a driving test and you might back up onto the pavement and turn to the examiner and say 'I'm nervous, I've never made that mistake before'. Looking at the examiner, you know immediately that you've failed and there is no point in carrying on the test. But you still carry on, disheartened. The examiner is looking at driving behaviour, he doesn't want to know that you're going through a stressful period or you have PMT. How would he know that you won't repeat that bad driving the next day or next week? So you show him that you are; confident, you know the highway code, you have concern for other road users, for pedestrians and you can handle the car and can use it in any situation and make decisions that are based on good practice.

Let's look at the driver's initial reaction, 'I'm nervous, I've never made that mistake before'. This might be the case however, a lot is being given away. The comment shows someone who is under-confident, is making excuses in order to manipulate a situation and is also showing a character trait perhaps that might be responsible for accidents in the future. What is said has not helped the situation. It is important not to put people's lives at risk and for drivers to show good practice.

Teachers are required to show good practice but there is no classroom code that includes strategies and skills. These are supposed to be gained on the job by experience and by watching the habits of those who are there already. Are those good models? At whose expense do teachers practice? Would it make sense to learn how to drive by watching others on the road? For both teaching and driving there are lives at risk, mistakes can make others' lives difficult.

Learning to Manage in the Classroom

As a trainee teacher in school your behaviour is a direct indication of how you can manage teaching. Mistakes made can make a difference in someone's learning so *how* you teach is important. You might lose control, shout because the children get too loud and present a fraught situation. You may go over to the tutor and say, 'Sorry, they are a problem today and I think it's because you are here.'

It is also not unusual for teachers to put the blame fully on the children, moving the spotlight from who is in control to those who haven't got their own controls. But as we know, children take their lead from the adult and can only develop correct behaviours with a lot of structure and support. Also when a problem arises for a student teacher, the brain bank of information that the student searches that may help solve the problem seems to be closed or empty of suggestions. Whilst the idea of curriculum has taken priority in the minds of educators, the skills and strategies have been undermined. A practised teacher is able to reflect on past similar situations, think about what has not worked, create a new response, think it through and keep it ready for the next time. For example, you know that when you say, 'Be quiet children and listen,' that some won't, or pencils will be dropped. So do it in order. Say 'Stop'. Say, 'Put your pencils away'. Say, 'Look at me.' 'Listen.' In this way, you have given the children direct actions to do and, one at a time so that all the children can follow them. It is as important to differentiate your directions as your lessons. A trainee teacher depends for the most part on the goodwill of the children, observation of other teachers, past experience of teachers known and a well prepared lesson. Sometimes however there are other factors that don't help. First lack of confidence or imagination in planning contingencies for '. . . if this happens, what I will do is . . .' Second, trainee teachers have little prior knowledge of the children and should be aware that the children are not always full of goodwill towards teachers and have their own agendas. The teachers being observed may have their own problems, or have found their own ways of holding the children's attention, which may not work for a trainee. However well prepared the lesson, teaching it may prove a different matter.

Contingency Planning

How and what do you prepare to be ready for the day?

- long-term academic plans
- short-term objectives
- motivational content for children
- resources listed and ready
- differentiated work prepared
- variety of approaches and presentation of work

- individual behaviour plans and class organization — where and how
- are your records up to date?

Are you happy with your planning for the day? Are you doing things you enjoy? Will the children pick up your enthusiasm? (remember adult as model)

You need to think to yourself, from the perspective of the observer, how will my behaviour be interpreted? What different behaviours can I present that show that I am aware of that perspective? Is my behaviour promoting good listening and learning? Am I rewarding the children enough?

How Do You Present Yourself?

- Are you happy with the way you look? comfortable? (Relaxed but ready presentation.)
- You will not sit at the desk but move around slowly. (Show that you know the mechanics of the room.)
- Give directions confidently making sure that everyone has heard. If the children are moving into groups make sure they know that you are giving each group four minutes extra to start them in the right direction. (Remind them of the schedule as you move from group to group.)
- Know where everything is in the room so that you can direct children to resources without much difficulty (unusual because you have made sure that everything that will be needed is easily available.)
- Make sure all the children know that you know what they are doing and what you are doing. (Talk quietly to the children, pace your way so that they all know where you are and don't have to shout out for your attention.)
- Know the children's names and show that you are interested in them individually and as members of a group. (Name their strengths and praise them for it, or a weakness that they are overcoming.)
- Try not to shout, one shout leads to another longer and louder. (If noise is getting too much, give the children something to do, 'put down your pencils and listen quietly'. Choose a behaviour they can do rather than, 'stop the noise or listen to me'.)
- Show that you and the children are working together (help them, teach them, listen to them, praise them, make things with them, be actively involved).
- Remember the small things and make them big. (Line up well, go in and out with the children, encourage good social interchanges, ask children to be helpful.)
- Know that this is everyday not just a special day. (Start as you mean to go on.)
- If you have given some children targets or group targets make sure you are checking on them consistently.

- Please remember that teaching comes before your need to finish making something that you want for a display. If a problem arises, or a question is asked, active teaching must come first.

What Impression Do You Make?

- Someone who is in control but not dogmatic and aggressive.
- Someone who has planned not just for today but for time to come.
- Someone who knows the classroom and has expectations for all the children.
- Someone who is unconcerned about having an observer but is sensitive to the difficult job of having to observe.
- Someone who is somewhat nervous but has overcome this by being ready and informed.
- Someone who knows that organization in classroom is necessary for training up good learning skills.
- Someone who is conscious of having ways of solving problem behaviours presenting in the classroom and is ready for them.
- Someone who is sensitive to children's needs and can talk and listen to those needs.

What Should Be the Contents of a Behaviour Policy for a School?

We move on from the individual to considering whole school policy. Setting up a behaviour policy should have three important features. It should explore a structure for management, a structure that will help the cohesion of staff and children. Schools need to look at all their options, cover all possible contingencies and remember positive ingredients. Make sure there are ways of initiating a forum for exploring issues for on-going review and revising. And most important is the way you will encourage, interchange, communicate, in a system in which teachers can share information. Talking about facets of education and stimulating discussion should keep the staffroom alive and not a place for escape. Teaching should not be just a job but a profession and an interest.

Behaviour is not just a question of devising a programme and sticking stickers. The art of being a teacher is recognizing that behaviour is long term, it is about knowing how people learn and if not, why not? Coping with behaviour and being in control is about awareness and about sharing information. It is about considering all the possibilities: What is the child telling you, from his or her behaviour? If the child wants attention when will you give it? Have you shared the information with others? Behaviour is about learning, it is complex and deserves a place, an important place, in the school.

Curriculum is what teachers do anyway. There are guidelines and knowing what you teach is important. But far more important, and the mark of a good school, are teachers knowing how to teach and receiving support from each other and from management.

What to Include in a School Policy

Setting up a school policy takes time and this is a scarce commodity for teachers, but rather than continue in the old ways, introducing new ideas can lead to renewed interest. A headteacher and staff need to make time to co-ordinate the aims and objectives of a behaviour policy for the whole school.

What do you want to include in your policy?

- positive approaches,
- time-out,
- exclusion-inclusion policy,
- smiley charts,
- individual programmes,
- token/reward systems,
- weekly meetings,
- steering committees,
- behaviour groups,
- social skills groups,
- focused learning groups,
- early skills groups,
- team teaching,
- integrated days for behaviour and learning,
- training on changing teaching habits.

Should there be fewer rules, stronger rules, circle times, individual long term programmes, peer group support? What suits your school? What suits your staff?

These could all be part of a policy but the school does not necessarily have to be dependent on one thing. All children and adults are different and a whole school is different and needs to look at itself carefully and choose what to do. A focus should never be on the problem, that is the indicator, the focus should be on the future plan, what to do now and where it will lead in the future.

Remember when you want to change, the change should be systematic, strategic and structural.

Structure

It is an important management move to form a structure in the school that bonds everyone in a common understanding. The important aspect is that everyone knows what everyone else is doing and everyone is supportive of each other. Where behaviour is concerned, there is sharing. In my present school there is a structure called the Token Economy System. This particular system would not suit every place but its principles can be adapted to suit other places. With that system are entities that are known to all the staff, the tokens, the giants (cheques), the bum bags, the record books, the saver and so on. The system also has names that the players recognize as 'in-talk'. Along with that comes a cognitive approach to target setting and the jargon that that entails. The children also learn more of the language of behaviour by describing what they need to achieve. All people in a system need to share a language. The most important function of our system is that children are always working for the next good thing. So the accent is positive. You might say we have a 'positive' programme but that is one aspect of a greater whole. We do not accept the prescriptive approaches as we discussed to start with. Assertive discipline is prescriptive but does it fit all occasions and all people? Does it fit your school ethos?

Positive Systems to Encourage Good Behaviour

Let's take the principle of working toward good things. On a course recently, an experienced teacher felt that after years of teaching, she had finally come up against a child who did not conform to her controls and failed to assimilate into her usually productive classroom. Being part of the management of the school, she felt she would be seen as not coping and was having doubts about her own abilities. She had instigated a tick and cross chart and wanted to know about sanctions and felt she had achieved a certain amount but that the system was not quite correct. Every fifteen minutes the child received a tick or cross. At break times, the child visited the headteacher who felt the visit was rewarding. On reflection from the course however, she thought that she was not rewarding abundantly enough. She was not being pleased enough with the child. How can the system work?

- Ticks are all right because they can be rewarding and rewarded. But crosses add a dimension that makes the system questionable. What do too many crosses mean, when there are also ticks? What does the child think when s/he sees a lot of crosses? Where do you go when the weight of crosses far exceeds the ticks, do you get into bigger and bigger sanctions?
- The answer is not to have crosses at all. They are unnecessary. What an adult is looking at is a single factor, is the child doing as requested? Is the request reasonable and can it successfully be achieved by the child? The only response to be charted will be the tick. In this way a graph can be made each day showing the amount of good times and the child has only one idea in his or her head and is not confused.

> If something is not right, the teacher's job is to help the child to get it right.

- Rewarding is easy. It is never harmful to a child. Sanctions are hard and most teachers cannot think of any in a hurry. Should this same child run out of the classroom, any sanction will prolong non co-operation.
- The answer is that the sanction has to be turned around, so that it is a reward that is not earned. For example, if the child enjoys the computer, s/he earns five minutes on it at the end of the day if s/he stays in the class. The teacher can help by reminding the child, by talking about new programmes or favourite programmes, by having a picture of the computer on the door with the child's name and the time s/he can use it.

We talked about these components of a programme and ended by suggesting that the headteacher continued to be involved and to make it important for the child to succeed. If a child is asking for attention, why not give it? Is asking for attention always a bad thing? We all do it and feel grateful when we receive it. As time goes on, giving attention can move to lesser attention as part of a planned part of a child's programme.

The most important factor was to recognize that the child must be prepared to be managed in the next class and it is important that teachers help each other within a school by preparing children and ensuring that the receiving teacher is part of the planning of good programmes to continue on through the school.

Setting up a Token Economy System

To get a system such as the Token Economy System up and running takes a great deal of planning and co-operation from staff. The system can take seven years to put into place and will still be added to and reflected upon in order for it to develop further to suit the changing needs of staff, school and children. Like behaviour, a strong system takes time and is built on firm principles.

Some staff needed convincing, but in the long run no member of staff would like to see a good working system go. It is hard to change habits and to work as a team but it is has to encompass all staff or no system will work efficiently. No system should become and remain as it is first conceived. It is reflected on, revised and amended. An important aspect of a system for staff, is that anyone can take over a problem a child is having. No one person is a god with more control than any other person. In this way, the child does not manipulate the adults and another adult does not lose face if s/he wants someone else to carry on with a child if the problem is big. Children recognize that all adults know their needs and that everyone works together.

To set up a system, you need to have a collegiate attitude in your school. The bureaucratic model does not lend itself to making a policy on behaviour that is chosen by everyone and put into practice by everyone. However, a strong management team means that the organization can support the staff and children within the policy that everyone understands.

Motivating and Training for Raising Standards of Intervention

If we could stop the world and start again, we might be able to think and plan long-term with freshness and foresight. Education and social actions are inextricably linked: education is basic to life. The world around us is evolving, so subtly that we are often unaware of the fact, and education is part of this great change.

Prevention of poor learning behaviour should be part of a conscious intervention in early education and teacher training. We can't stop what is already past, but we can plan for the future. I can only see and contribute to, not a simple response to what is happening, but a long-term thinking about how to make early initiatives in helping children and teachers to adjust to future educational, behavioural and social conditions.

The daily routine, responses and recording of curriculum seems in recent years to have taken away the 'joy' of teaching for many. The elements of teaching that consisted of knowing whether a child has reached a certain stage in which to embark on the next skills or strategy for learning, that stimulated the teacher in the next day to see if it had indeed occurred, the process of behavioural development from dependence learning to independent learning, all seem to have shrunk into mediocrity.

Discourse should be encouraged about how teachers teach, how teachers approach those children who have complex learning difficulties, and how teachers can teach the children behaviours and learning behaviours that will help them in their future years. The days of giving teachers prescriptions for managing behaviour, for giving smiley faces that confines intervention and looks to short-term results, must give way to a more professional teacher, an educationalist who understands when a child presents behavioural difficulties and begins a conversation that plans for the way the child should be rather than to change what the child is doing now. Education must be seen as a process among many people and not a momentary input by one. This is not extra work for teachers to do. It should be an intrinsic part of what teachers are and what they are trained to know.

Challenging behaviour does not suddenly start, it develops and contorts depending on what it meets and how it is met from the very beginnings. The early factors cannot be changed, indeed the nature of life and the colour in life *are* the differences. What educationalists can do is to recognize those signs early on and approach them with vision and in communication with those persuasive and influential factors in the child's life, the years of education.

In the same way, there should be recognition early of the needs of teachers in training and teachers who are already practising. Teachers need to be encouraged into being more ambitious and to feel confident about using skills to manage the complex difficulties within the classroom. Teachers must be motivated to understand the idea of long-term intervention and how each teacher is only one small part in the continuum of a child's education. A teacher needs to be motivated, to be interested in the process, to be creative within that and to be aware of his/her own strengths. Motivating and training teachers go hand in hand, teachers need to know that they are recognized as professionals.

A quote from a teacher at a recent conference was that teachers were with children all the time and didn't want to discuss children at break or in the lunch time. I was sorry to hear this because in a sense not speaking means that there is no sharing of all those possibly exciting, possibly annoying, possibly frightening things happening in the classroom. It is important that there is continual talk about the children in or out of class and the school environment should be an arena for the sharing and pooling of expertise that improves the work with the children and the expertise of the school. But this has to develop, it has to be arrived at through a response to the children's needs and to the needs of those working with difficult children.

The first important element is that the management team are at one regarding the importance of training. How to work with children who need a great deal of intervention needs particular skills and more importantly the academic understanding. All staff should be considered for courses that will not only benefit the school but also the individual as personal confidence is essential in sustaining quality intervention. Staff should be encouraged to take more than a cursory glance at the children in their care, they should be aware of and understand all the facets of the child's difficulties and to be actively involved in sharing their intervention with others and with the child. Because of that, interest can be infectious and can grow. Stimulating thought means making a positive working environment. Motivating teachers and staff is about being excited about what we do, about not being content about going in one direction but increasing the directions in which we are looking to help the children. So how are staff motivated to want to continue to study as well as working full time?

Motivating Teachers

This book is written from the viewpoint of a teacher of children with special needs, but the issue of motivation affects all teachers and schools. It means that the energy and excitement of what teachers do should be present in the school agenda, although it cannot be formulated as a policy, but is at the heart of all matters.

Motivation encourages staff to look for new ways of managing problems within the school and to make long-term plans for solving them. It is the accompanying discussion that helps teachers to find ways to help children, and this can be translated into school policy. It means being involved in increasing teachers' concerns about teaching; how they understand what they are undertaking in school.

If a teacher is within a training institution then s/he is aware of the latest thinking behind the issues of teaching children with challenging behaviours and this may be passed on to schools. In an ideal world, teachers in schools would have links with the training institutions who are formulating new ideas for improving behaviour management. Giving a teacher a sense of personal esteem is part of being more professional and of being valued and a thinking teacher is more likely to have a successful system in class than one who is controlling by task and subject alone. The motivation should come from the management team who ought to have access to the latest thinking on developing learning behaviours. They should be encouraging teachers to want to understand, as well as to teach children. The motivation of staff is intrinsically bound up with teaching the children and so the issue of motivation is one that travels down through the whole school. Teachers who are confident and sharing have the vision of the continuum of intervention that raises the standards of the working environment.

Training follows motivation, improves the levels of understanding and the work of the teacher with the children presenting difficult behaviours.

Training for Planning and Development

A utopian world you think? Perhaps, but everyone needs to practise their part of this continuum of education. There should be training in organizing long-term programmes, where the next person knows that a child is just beginning to play and therefore is encouraged to play in a group in the next year so that all the children benefit. It may be that at present exclusion is the only ultimate sanction, but it would be positive to feel that early intervention for the child and the teacher in training may coincide to make education a shared experience. The curriculum is well documented — now how about a long look at how teachers teach and how teachers help children to acquire learning and social behaviours that make the delivery of curriculum possible? Teachers shouldn't be responding to problems, they should be planning long-term interventions, motivating staff, training staff and sharing the responsibilities of providing a long-term vision of education for each child within each social grouping.

Organizing long-term programmes is about prevention and planning, and about purpose. It is about motivating teachers to want to know about how to develop good behaviours and how to keep an enquiring mind. Training is about developing ways of thinking within a rich educating environment, where teachers can be motivated, trained and be able to put theory into practice and know that what they have learned will work. Motivating is about having time to discuss all those small happenings in the classroom that are crucial in the relationship between teachers and children. My own school is planning to continue this idea in contributing to the training of teachers and in the early recognition and remediation of children with challenging behaviours.

Reviewing the Key Issues in the Management of Behaviour in Schools

Language

We have said earlier that children are not developing good language constructs, and for many concepts and cognitive functioning are not in place and therefore cause many misunderstandings and behavioural difficulties, either because the child is not listening and unable to follow the adult reasoning, or because the child responds inappropriately which causes a negative response from the adult. Let's look again at a simple example. A class was comparing the life of the Greeks to that of the Tudors. The word the teacher used was civilizations. Ideas were teased from the children but when asked what civilization was at the end, the children were mystified. The context was not enough to help them.

Quite often teachers may say, 'You are being rude'. The child may smile. The smile may be defensive because the description is misunderstood. It may even have a laughing connotation for the child. Before lessons, teachers may look at the words they are going to use and make sure that children know what a 'hoof' is or a 'country' or 'a plus sign'. In the same way, teachers must be sure that children know what the words used in class or school rules are. The rules should be positive; not, 'Do not walk on the furniture' but 'Keep my feet on the floor', not 'Do not make a noise here' but 'Do be quiet here'. Rules should be few and consistent and simply worded. Children do need to be reminded frequently.

These changes may seem small and ineffectual, however, in the long term it make adults think about what they are saying to children. It is better to say, 'How do we behave here . . . quietly . . . can you whisper that word?' It is harder to ask a child to show 'not making a noise', or 'show me what we are not supposed to do!' Part of a good school policy is to make people think about showing children what to do rather than saying what they should not do. You cannot ask a child to show you what they should not do!

Earlier, language and disorders of language were talked about and whole school policy can reflect an understanding of this.

Working Together in a Structure

In the end you should have a greater awareness of and be stimulated into considering, as a staff, how to have a collegiate approach to managing the idea of behaviour. Many schools still have teachers who must hide in classrooms and pretend not to have any problems of discipline. The old tricks don't always work and then quite often teachers use the structure to threaten children, 'go to the headteacher' and so on. A structure is not a big disciplinary machine run by management. It should be a thinking team, sharing technical skills and moving together to help children in need and motivate those who are forging ahead. We all need to take into account knowing about children and the various developmental states and the basic laws of behaviour, individually and in groups.

Share Understandings of Children's Difficulties

If attention is poor in a small proportion of each class what is wrong with organizing an attention group where for fifteen minutes a week a specialised system and resources are used to train up attention. You will be surprised by the improvements, but also the knowledge that a development takes place over months relieves the stress that is common in dealing with the area of behaviour. Action research would be a good method of looking at the viability of such a scheme.

A Time and Place to Talk

So ideas? What ideas have you got off the top of your head that have been festering for months but have been so unusual as to seem impossible? Discussion about behaviour is endless and it should bring people together. At home, at work, wherever people meet and mingle, behaviour provides a fascinating topic of conversation.

Consider staff behaviour, can you talk to each other? In the end, there is no substitute for teachers who are willing to work as a team on the children's behalf and who maintain flexibility, tolerance, a sense of humour and a belief in colleagues and even the most challenging children.

Ofsted and Behaviour Policy

What does an Ofsted inspection include under behavioural expectations?

Pupils' Attitudes to Learning, Their Behaviour and Attendance

In particular, 'inspectors must evaluate and report on pupils' response to the teaching and other provision made by the school, highlighting any weakness . . .' This is significant to teachers in the context of behaviour management. Judgments will be made specifically at:

- pupils' attitudes to learning,
- pupils' behaviour, including the incidence of exclusions,
- the quality of relationships in the school, including their contributions to the life of the community and
- other aspects of pupils' personal development, including their contributions to the life of the community. (Ofsted, 1995)

Managing a Behaviour Policy in School

Suggestions for managing a behaviour policy in school may take the form of the following:

- A group should be formed to co-ordinate the ideas of the staff. This group should contain members of the management team, representatives from the class teachers, the SEN co-ordinator, a class assistant/playground assistant and representative parent if possible. (Dependent on the number of volunteers in the school.)

  1 Should meet once a fortnight minimally, during which time individuals will work on areas of responsibility within the policy.
  2 Should disseminate written information to staff for ratification at staff meetings.

- General interest areas should have definite procedures and rules which all staff should adhere to.

  1 These include: playtimes, early mornings, moving around the school, lunch times, end of the day.
  2 General behaviour expectations should be laid down for the classroom.
  3 Year 6 should recognize behaviour expectations using group contracts, formalized expectations and a consciousness about being models for the other children in the school.
  4 Individual programmes should be written and circulated before staff meetings for discussion, modifications and acceptability. Programmes should be shared with staff who are in contact with the child and should fit into a five week schedule and be assimilated into an overall school programme.
  5 General observation sheets that are user-friendly should be devised.

- All plans should be made clear to the children. Posters can be made with expectations, and assemblies can stress the suitable types of behaviour in school.

- All staff should be sympathetic to colleagues and share ideas and matters such as organization of time, planning ahead, details and resources.

- Time, resources and staff should have a certain amount of time within a week to share: perhaps groups that need tasks that train up attention or listening skills. The SEN could be involved here.

Additional Considerations

- SEN to consider all children who have difficulty maintaining attention to task or have poor listening skills for a long-term special group. Teacher to back up skills by practising them in the classroom.
- Staff should see that it is positive to voice concerns as long as s/he is prepared to put forward possible ways around a problem or ask for other input.
- Sticker charts should be discussed and seen as a whole school response and process rather than an individual activity in the classroom. A behaviour policy only works with the enthusiasm of all staff throughout the year.
- Programmes should be organized simply so that they can be sustained by the adults with review periods.
- Whole school behaviour language could include a few of the following so that children have certain behaviours to work toward and understand what they mean; politeness, helpfulness, enthusiasm, showing good concentration, ability to work well, sitting down, co-operating with peers, attentiveness, following directions, working in pairs, kindness, awareness of others' needs, being non-aggressive. Hopefully, as many of these have already been observed, role models already exist within the school.
- If inappropriate behaviours are observed such as throwing pencils, sharpening pencils, running around corridors first thing in the morning, over-organizing other children, then these children are not understanding social messages. How can these behaviours be turned into appropriate behaviours? What motivation do these children have to develop behaviours that will be stressed within your school?
- Midday assistants need a short course on the unwritten elements of the job of midday assistant.
- Teaching staff need to see playtimes as a valuable teaching period in the school day.

Conclusion

All schools need to work together. Figure 11.1 shows, ideally, the major support processes in the management of behaviour. The chart is used as a training resource in induction and for management courses at my present school.

Figure 11.1: *Key issues in the management of behaviour in mainstream schools* (Burnard, 1995 — use as a training resource)

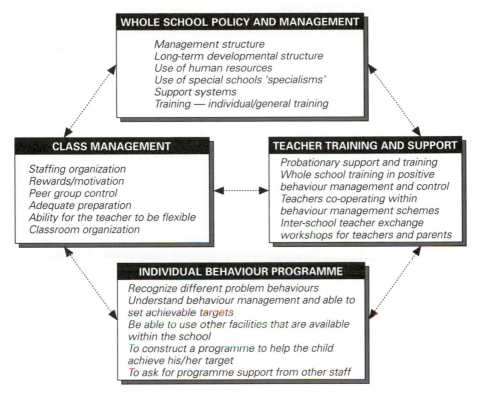

WHOLE SCHOOL POLICY AND MANAGEMENT

Management structure
Long-term developmental structure
Use of human resources
Use of special schools 'specialisms'
Support systems
Training — individual/general training

CLASS MANAGEMENT

Staffing organization
Rewards/motivation
Peer group control
Adequate preparation
Ability for the teacher to be flexible
Classroom organization

TEACHER TRAINING AND SUPPORT

Probationary support and training
Whole school training in positive behaviour management and control
Teachers co-operating within behaviour management schemes
Inter-school teacher exchange workshops for teachers and parents

INDIVIDUAL BEHAVIOUR PROGRAMME

Recognize different problem behaviours
Understand behaviour management and able to set achievable targets
Be able to use other facilities that are available within the school
To construct a programme to help the child achieve his/her target
To ask for programme support from other staff

It is important that good behaviour on the part of the staff is observed and that it is understood that children's progress is seen as a continuum and that problems should be discussed. Supporting each other and the children makes a stronger school. Training staff can improve teachers' performance, by knowing and putting that knowledge into practice. Having policies that raise the self esteem of staff and children is a way forward for all schools.

12   An Overview

Introduction

If children are to manage our world in the future then they need to be equipped to do so. Not all children will grow peacefully and contentedly. Some children from almost their first breath present problems. The caring adults may respond spontaneously, and unconsciously develop a need in the child to manage his own worlds in ways that are different from others. At times these are anti-social ways that will present the child as a problem to himself in which his reactions from others will always be negative and which he may then seek out re-interring his self-image. Other children may have similar reactions from their carers and yet they may develop more positively and with other strategies to help them face the world. Surprisingly, children having the same mothering and fathering do not present similar behaviours. After all they have a different pecking order, variable physical characteristics, different experiences or similar experiences with different interpretations. The expression, 'it was a hard act to follow' is about the impossibility of sameness, and says nothing about the strength of difference. Sometimes people's expectations can create stress for some members of a family and similarly for members of the class who find it difficult to keep in line with the higher achievers in any part of the curriculum. Giving all children credit for their strengths and working encouragingly with their weaknesses is part of balancing the equation of the classroom.

Behavioural Awareness in Schools

Understanding that knowing about behaviour helps to understand knowing the multi-faceted classroom is crucial for a teacher. In a course on *Behavioural Awareness in Schools*, which I presented recently, a Newly Qualified Teacher (NQT) related the usual tale of 'half an hour given in my training for the most important feature of being a teacher'. She had had a great struggle with so many difficulties and had no strategies to call on. She had little support and had not had her contract renewed. She bemoaned the fact that she had not had this course before. Other members of the course said that in the three days, their heads were spinning with ideas to put theory into practice. Knowing that all activity in the classroom could be seen as hidden learning behaviour was important to this group. Recognizing, for instance, that it was not *what* children learnt but *how* they learnt, and how that gave them skills to learn more was the crucial element in the classroom. As an example, sitting at a table doing a maths worksheet independently meant that the child had

- listened to directions and past instructions,
- had shared the learning with a group of other children,
- could concentrate on a task without losing direction,
- had learnt to put up his/her hand and to wait for help,
- could press lightly on the pencil so as not to break the nib,
- could ask another child to pass the rubber,
- was motivated intrinsically to finish, and
- extrinsically in that all the group could have the class ball at playtime if they all managed during maths, knew where the abacus was and could ask to get it without causing a problem for any other child.

Everything a child does and every situation s/he is in, either consolidates behaviour or teaches new behaviours.

Even in the best possible world, not all teachers have an innate ability to control a class. Control for most is not an innate skill. This is not because of a lack of ability, but more likely to have been ineffectual training where the world of the classroom is not brought alive realistically and practically for the trainee. Even more emphasis on problem solving would come nearer the mark. For most students, the idea that they can consider more creative means to an end is unheard of. Sometimes even the simplest answer is considered: a teacher is so busy that s/he forgets to look at the children's eyes when talking to them, each one. What teacher is not guilty of this kind of behaviour? S/he looks over heads or to the task in hand, talking while doing. It is no wonder that so many children abandon their normal attention behaviour for the more annoying type of attention seeking. We all crave attention; how do you feel in social situations when people walk past you, talk to others, don't listen to your whole sentence or have a conversation whilst busily doing another task? Do you feel important, or do you wonder whether the information that the other person is giving, or that you are sharing, is important enough to remember? Being a teacher is knowing that what you are saying is important and who you are saying it to is important.

Motivation Towards Improving Behaviour

> I thought, this child has been good last week I shall give this child a certificate if he can sit in his seat at least for the first ten minutes of each day this week. So I went to the child and explained it to him. But I could tell it wasn't important and he didn't care so I didn't bother after that. His behaviour got worse, so I wouldn't have been able to give it to him anyway.

A teacher on a course told me this story. My reply would surprise no-one. A teacher or adult is the person who makes a situation and makes it work. The certificate was a great idea and the child needed convincing, but clearly the teacher needed convincing first.

She needed to work out a schedule for the child,

- to present it well,
- make it seem attractive,
- put the child in situations where it would work, and
- praise and give intermittent encouragement.

It was necessary to make working for the certificate seem important because some children do not have a vision of success, the adult has to keep it and share it.

The classroom is an exciting place. Time goes very fast and not everything planned can be finished on time. Life in a classroom is on-going, it is developing time, and exploring time. Early behaviour, learning and social behaviour, is all happening and the most important person to a child can be any adult who is involved with them and helping them in the right direction. Learning respect is about modelling. Respect from adults to adults and to children is quickly picked up by the child. Adults in the school need to show that they are learning as well and to show good learning behaviours. An adult should listen, should walk down the corridors, should talk to children and colleagues with interest, should be pleased to accompany the child to the playground and to ask what they will play, and even help them. A teacher may also use a few early sessions of classroom time on learning playground skills. What is important to an adult will be watched by the child.

More personally, adults in school need to be open to suggestions about their own practice. They need to use to advantage their own history, development and interests. They need to be able to ask questions and develop the ability to reflect on past practice and to be self-critical to advantage. They need to have control of their own behaviour and thoughts. They need to have information about the whole structure and a vision of how to work within it and with it. Understanding how you work yourself, improves teacher confidence.

Important Elements in the Process of Learning

This is a suitable point to re-emphasize the process:

1. The curriculum is what all teachers teach, prepare, organize the subject, demonstrate, discuss, encourage, direct and record.
2. The curriculum is the tent. The foundation of the tent contains the 'teaching' factors, the essential ingredients, the skills, the strategies, the knowledge about how children learn, and how to develop behaviours that will promote learning. Not what it is, but why and how form the structure of teaching.

3   Recognizing the way to communicate to children; the language you
     use to train up understanding and the language they use to show how
     they are understanding.
4   Recognizing that the children come to school with all their own bag-
     gage from their early years. The outcome of those early years is in
     evidence when a child hits school, s/he goes public. Teachers cannot
     change any of that but can build in schools' behaviours and informa-
     tion that helps the child to rationalize and manage the past and present
     and develop a future.

Passing Items to Consider

The focus on the curriculum and its delivery causes undue stress to teachers
who are seeing that the practical aspects of teaching, their relationships and
control of the children must be in place. Professionalism in teachers must mean
knowing about the art of teaching and about those they serve, the children.
We should consider the real side of teaching, the aspects that most teachers
see as reality. Targeting behaviour is often spoken about and should never be
an afterthought or an additional problem centred on one child — it should be
a whole class/school policy.

Teachers report feeling constant criticism over delivering the curriculum
whilst they work hard daily on all the other aspects of teaching. These aspects
they call the real problems in teaching, not the paperwork involved in the curriculum. Reports sent home nowadays often merely outline coverage of the
national curriculum. Sometimes the personal achievements of the child and
how they have learnt are no longer part of the report.

When facing problem behaviour, which can take up so much of a teacher's
time, the following points may be borne in mind:

- If you find you are saying a child 'always does this behaviour . . .' get
  in first and arrange matters so that the problem behaviour does not get
  a chance. If there is behaviour that promotes learning, reward it.
- Be determined to make a course of action work. If you decide a child
  needs to work for a certificate get the child excited, train up a need
  for the certificate, don't say 'he didn't seem interested and his behaviour got worse.' False promises ruin any programme.
- If you don't like a child who taps on the table, train the child to put
  up his hand instead. Your training may solve the problem.
- Restraint may be appropriate. Some children have never had their
  hand held by an adult and felt a comforting control. Maybe the parent
  doesn't bother, or uses the hand as a negative means of control.
- Sometimes you need to train up just holding a hand to help the child
  towards independent control.

- If a child seems likely to hurt himself or others, make sure there is another adult available to help with the situation.
- Look to your school's or LEA's policy on restraint.

Some Questions or Activities You Might Like to Ask or Do

1 Share with your colleagues any difficulties that you face in your classroom.
2 Think of the control words that you currently use in your room or around school. Which ones are the most effective in gaining pupil attention?
3 When having difficulties in the classroom or playground where do you go to verbalize your concerns? If you find it difficult to verbalize your concerns, think about why it is difficult.
4 Have you ever changed your behaviour to accommodate a plan? How did this feel and could you sustain it?
5 How do you respond independently to behaviours in your room, classroom, playground or anywhere around school or how do you make specific plans and share them with the whole staff?
6 Do you start smiley faces charts, and then drop them? Or do you finish them with relief? Or do you find that everyone has lost interest? Or do you see them as a whole programme with contingencies to success? If not in the classroom, how do you reward children around the school when they are managing?
7 Solving problems in the classroom should be a long-term plan with short concise objectives. Do you know how to do this?
8 These are the children that I feel I know better than the other children. Why do I know them well?
9 The appropriate behaviours that I have recently observed around the school are. . . . have I encouraged them?
10 The inappropriate behaviours that I have recently observed around school are. . . . what did I do about them?
11 Who else could I involve in the management of the children that I am responsible for?
12 What would I have to change about myself and my own practices in order to accommodate a plan?
13 Are there areas in the school where a child can go to practice behaviours outside the classroom?

Think Objectively about the Strengths and Weaknesses of Your Own School

1 The school — What can you contribute to the school that will facilitate the making of a firm policy for behaviour management?

2 The classroom — What changes can you make to your own practices in order to be more aware of the interaction between adults and children within a system?

3 Communication with one another — What changes can you make in time and resources in order to communicate fears and successes with one another?

Remember

- Don't put yourself into situations you cannot follow through.
- Don't start a sentence 'If you don't, I'll . . .' Children recognize the lack of planning and immediate reaction. If you shout, it can only get louder . . . if you punish, it gets worse.

For the most part children are asking the adult to solve problems for them, because they don't know the answers. If they cannot understand the rules, they will behave in such a way to demonstrate that. When a child hits school, the child goes public. Adapting is variable for all children and each one has little idea of future needs, it is the adult who has to have the foresight. Behaviour systems for children and schools take time and consideration to produce. Stress in teaching is caused by the need to show immediate results and this may mean that children with difficulties are excluded from situations even at the beginnings of school. Taking them away from situations they can't manage means they won't learn and practise good behaviours. As time passes, they don't recognize how good things can be or feel the desire to work for the rewards. A child learns to resent the activities or things s/he can't have.

Conclusion

Helping children is a shared experience. If a child is having a difficult time remember you are not the one with the problems. Try to solve the child's problem and if you can't, ask another colleague to talk through ideas for managing the problem. Support each other in the best interests of the child. All those children are journeying over cobbled stones and difficult terrain, they need to be eased towards futures that we cannot predict.

References

BURNARD, S. (1986) 'Good Companions: A Combination of Psychotherapy and Parent Training used in Families with a Severely Handicapped Child', paper presented at Third World Congress on Infant Psychiatry and Allied Disciplines, Stockholm.

BURNARD, S. and YAXLEY, H. (1996) 'The never-ending story: Reflection and development', in O'HANLON, C. (ed.) *Professional Development through Action Research in Educational Settings*, London: Falmer Press.

BURNARD, S. and NESBITT, H. (1995) 'Teaching, learning and researching together in a residential primary school for emotionally disturbed children', *European Journal of Special Needs*, **10**, 3, pp. 258–82, London: Routledge.

BURNER, J.S., OLVER, R.R. and GREENFIELD, P.M. (eds) (1966) *Studies in Cognitive Growth*, New York: Wiley.

CONTACT A FAMILY 16 Strutton Ground, London, SW1 P2HP.

COOPER, P. and IDEUS, K. (eds) (n.d.) Attention Deficit Hyperactivity Disorder: Medical, Educational and Cultural Issues, obtained from, Allam Rimmer, Charlton Court, East Sutton, Near Maidstone, Kent, ME17 3DQ.

COOPER, P. and UPTON, G. (1992) 'Ecosystemic approach to classroom behaviour problems', in WHELDALL, K. (ed.) *Discipline in Schools: Psychological Perspectives on the Elton Report*, London: Routledge.

ELLIOT, J. (1991) *Action Research for Educational Change-developing Teachers and Teaching*, Milton Keynes: Open University Press.

ELTON REPORT (1989) *Department of Education and Science*, London: HMSO.

FISH, D. (1988) *Learning through Practice in Initial Teacher Training*, London: Kogan Page Ltd.

IDEUS, K. and COOPER, P. (1995) 'Chemical cosh or therepeutic tool: Towards a balanced view of the use of stimulant medication with children diagnosed with attention deficit/hyperactivity disorder', *Therepeutic Care and Education*, **4**, 3, pp. 52–63.

KEMMIS, R. (1980) 'Action Research in Retrospect and Prospect: Mimeo', presented at the Annual General Meeting of the Australian Association for Research, Sydney, November.

LOVETT, T.C. (1973) 'Self management projects with children with learning difficulties', *Journal of Learning Disabilities*, pp. 138–50.

OFSTED (1995) *Framework for the Inspection of Schools*, London: HMSO.

PIAGET, J. (1955) *Language and Thought of the Child*, New York: Meridian.

WHELDALL, K. (1992) *Discipline in Schools Psychological Perspectives on the Elton Report*, London: Routledge.

WHITE, M. (1996) *Raining Self Esteem*, Dunstable, Beds: Folens Ltd.

WITT, J., ELLIOT, S.N. and GRESHAM, F.M. (1988) *Handbook of Behaviour Therapy in Education*, New York, London: Plenum Press.

WORLD HEALTH ORGANISATION (1994) The ICD-10 Classification of Mental and Behavioural Disorders.

Index